332.678 Fri
Frishberg, Daniel
Escape from the herd : secrets
from the super rich /

34028072452049
SM $14.95 ocm74751966
07/06/09

D0912261

Escape from the Herd:
Secrets of the Super Rich

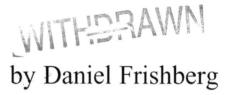

by Daniel Frishberg

and

Laura A. Baker

Foreword by Tobin Smith

Presented to
Spring Branch Memorial Library

By

**The City of
Hunters Creek Village**

Harris County
Public Library
your pathway to knowledge

Cover design by Rebecca Price
www.rebeccaprice.com

Escape from the Herd:
Secrets of the Super Rich

By Daniel Frishberg

and

Laura A. Baker

© Copyright 2005 by Daniel Frishberg and Laura A. Baker
Printed in the United States of America

All rights reserved. No part of this book
may be reproduced in any manner
without permission of the
authors and the publisher.

Published by BizRadio Press
3050 Post Oak Blvd., Ste. 1680
Houston, TX 77056
www.escapefromtheherd.com

Printed in the United States of America
ISBN 0-9777549-2-8 $14.95

Escape from the Herd

Foreword by Tobin Smith

My good friend Dan Frishberg was one of the first people to ever put me on the radio. Now a few years later, I opened his book and discovered that he is again a first. Dan has taken a unique approach to discussing an important aspect of investing which very few people talk about, and that is human nature. I think that as a reader and as an investor, you can find a message here, and it is a message that rarely comes from the Wall Street world. On Wall Street most people are compensated for making transactions happen not compensated for the outcome of the transactions, and so they don't tend to bring that conversation to the table as Dan has done here.

I think that *Escape from the Herd* provides good ballast, a good weight to the plethora of advice out there that says that you always have to do this or this. One of the great points that Dan makes is that many times not doing anything is doing something. Doing nothing is an investment strategy!

When you make a decision to make an investment in something, to me, it has to be a really compelling reason. I say, "Nice to have or need to have?" I want a need-to-have. We know that the supply demand imbalance of natural gas or copper or new technologies are so compelling that we don't have to be particularly right about the price at which we buy this investment because we're going to be a little bit early.

I know that it's an unstoppable train. I know that the size of this business that I'm investing in is going to ultimately be many, many multiples of what it is today. I also know that human beings are on various curves of the early adopter and what Dan calls the herd. You know, the herd is really the mass market and I agree that any investment, which is massively compelling, is one that I'm making before the herd or anyone else knows about it. When we started making investments in VoIP or digital cameras or the Internet, the investment people thought the Internet was a two-way radio! I think they thought it was a fad. Those are the same people; the same "experts" who were saying the Internet is going to replace sex and Monday night football.

So, there's a very logical part of human nature and human behavior imbedded in investing. I come from the same perspective as Dan. I've been much more successful in my investing when I focus on the human issues and not on whether the P/E ratio is ten, fifteen, fifty or one-hundred.

Ultimately, there are repetitive features in human nature that if you're going to be an investor are going to allow you to make money and making money is the final thing. I keep score by making money and I think there are a lot of people who keep score by being right. They say, "I'm going to be right no matter what." When it comes to the investment business, there's only one way I know how to keep score and that is: Am I getting wealthy or meeting my financial goals?

The big struggle is not finding the right ideas. What Dan is saying in this very interesting, unusual book is the big struggle is over-coming yourself. If you get yourself out of the way, you'll do well. You don't need to own stocks 365 days of the year, decade after decade. There are very good reasons not to own them. There are very good reasons to own bonds, real estate and energy and to divest of traditional stocks. Listen to your own voice, not the roar of the crowd!

In the end, building wealth is really about two things. The first is being optimistic about the economy and freedom and democracy. The second part is really about human nature and that is the part that is the least talked about in the market and one of the most important aspects to investing: overcoming your own ego. This amusing, challenging first book by Dan Frishberg goes to the heart of the matter.

~ Toby

Escape from the Herd

Dedication

To the smartest, most fun kids on the planet, Stephanie,
Niki and Larry. You'll never know how much you
changed my life, and what a huge part of it you are.

To the beautiful Elisea, my inspiration, my role model,
my partner, and most of all my companion for life,
I can only say – It's been quite a ride!

Escape from the Herd

Acknowledgments

Thank you Al Kaleta, Rick Jordan and Karl Eggerss for being
smart and making me look smart all the time.

Thank you to our regular guests on the BizRadio show in no
particular order: (How do you rank giants?) Tobin Smith, John
Bollinger, John Murphy, Elaine Garzarelli, Michael Cox, Scott
Belieir, Mike Norman, Arnaud De Borchgrave, Henry Kissinger,
Tom Delay, Rick Perry, John Cornyn and Kay Bailey Hutchinson,
Dick Arms, Jack Welch, Col. Oliver North, Frank Cappiello,
Jeane Kirkpatrick, Joe Battipaglia, Mark Cuban, Harry Dent, John
Dessauer, Don King, Steve Forbes, Herb Greenberg, Dick Mor-
ris, George Muzea, Howard Simmons, Sid Ceasar, Deborah
Norville, Ed McMahon, Ted Koppel, Louis Navellier, Roger
Moore, Mario Gabelli, Mary Farrell, Howard Ruff, Geraldine
Ferraro, T. Boone Pickens, Jim Cramer, Robert Kiyosaki, John
Najarian and Pete Najarian, Harry Connick, Jr., William Shatner,
Dr. John Rutledge, Laura Miller, Dan Akroyd, Grover Norquist,
Scott Rasmusssen, Pat Sajak, Daisy Fuentes, Mel Tillis, Maury
Povich, Gene Simons, Brian Wesbury, Louie Anderson, Peter
Boyle, Richard Perle, Ralph Acampora, Frank Holmes, Bill
Payne, John Bott and John Vaughn and too many more to men-
tion: (Forgive me for not putting in their titles, which would
double the size of this acknowledgment) for putting us on the
map and making us first with the inside secrets from the front
line all these years.

Thank you to Laura Baker for bringing Franny Gold to the mix and for never running out of patience with my constant additions and changes.

Most importantly, thank you Pamela Caddell, Ella Rinn, Genevieve Casanova Cespedes, Mit Tai and the whole staff of Bizradio network led by Brent Clanton for keeping me alive while I do this work.

Secrets of the Super Rich

Escape from the Herd

Introduction

Before I was ten-years-old, a very wise old man used to point out to me that making money is the opposite of human nature. This is as true today as it was more than fifty-plus years ago when I first heard it. Probably because this reality has always been the lens through which I see the world, making money has always come easily to me.

I now understand that stocks and bonds and other types of paper or electronic deals seem very abstract to most people. Wars aren't fought over mutual funds or loan contracts; they are fought over land because almost everyone finds it easier to relate and understand "real" things. To me, the paper stuff is just as real and easy to grasp as the solid stuff. I don't know why, and I didn't really know until I was in the Marines at seventeen, that this was a gift everyone doesn't have.

People describe this gift as the ability to see where the money is. I always thought of it as just having a feel for people and how they behave. I've actually always suspected that most people just don't enjoy or care enough about other people to actually focus on them and their behavior.

Whatever the cause, the bottom line is this. Because of being good at this one thing I had the opportunity to be around many brilliant and fabulously successful people – sports heroes, famous entertainers and world-class political leaders. From these perennial winners, I've learned many important things, such as how to focus, how to create the results I want in my life and generally, how to find a way to win. In turn, these life skills, which do not come naturally to most of us, have made me a much more effective and a much wealthier investor.

After reading *Escape from the Herd* through the first time, I realized that I needed to bring in the questioning voice of a new investor. I asked my book collaborator, Laura Baker, a young woman and a new investor herself, to create a character who could be in dialogue with me. She came back with Franny Gold, the delightful and inquisitive massage therapist.

Franny Gold may be a fictitious character, but to say she doesn't exist is incorrect. This urbane, street-smart, beautiful, witty young masseuse represents a composite of my whole audience. She reacts to the insights in this book just as regular, smart, decent people do, and her questions, comments and confusion are the questions and confusion I find when I get questions from my radio audience.

Franny's responses represent the e-mails, the on-air calls and the questions people ask me when they recognize me at a party or on the tennis court.

Even though these insights don't come naturally to her, Franny, like you, is easily able to grasp them, when she finally confronts them.

I am writing this book primarily for people who live in the United States of America. As Americans, facing nothing but opportunity and plenty, Franny Gold and you will find that to make a lot more money, and to get a lot more out of our wonderful economy, all you have to do is to stop making a few key mistakes.

Escape from the Herd is my opportunity to pass on to you what I have learned during my fifty-plus years of studying both Wall Street and the human race. If the information in this book helps you get more of what you want, please pass it forward.

Escape from the Herd

Massage Session #1

Franny: He comes in on Thursday: a blue-eyed mensch with a shy smile who says he's Dan Frishberg, but I can call him The Moneyman. "OK, Dan The Moneyman," I say, "My name is Francisca Adreinne D'Ore, but everyone calls me Franny, Franny Gold. Take your clothes off and hop up on the table. I'll be back in a few." I leave him with a hot towel, candles, incense and listening to Enya. (They like it swank at The Club.)

So, there I am with Dan The Moneyman face down, and I ask him my usual question, "How did you make your money?" As a massage therapist, I hear a lot of stuff. I was not prepared, however, for this guy's answer *or* his cha cha cha delivery. There is something else, too: The truth is that I was shocked that he took me seriously. I mean he took *me* seriously. Like, I could be rich, too, or at least not have to sell Mary Kay when I'm eighty.

He starts talking and doesn't pause to breathe for the next thirty minutes. (This, by the way, is not an ideal for receiving a massage.) He's looking through the hole in the face cradle and speaking to my toes, but I can hear him just fine.

Dan: Are you using your elbow? It feels like a dowel! Ahhh, that's nice!

OK. You want my story? It goes like this: For thirty or forty

5

years, I had success investing in the market. Until 1995, I invested like an accountant. This was how I operated: I would buy if I could buy the company cheaper than I thought the stock was worth.

In the nineties, we came into a secular bull market – that's what we call it when the bull market lasts for a long, long time – and certain areas of the market like high-tech became lucrative and stock prices started to take off. Cheap stocks were staying cheap and expensive stocks grew more expensive. Investing like an accountant stopped working for me, but I kept doing it anyway. I wasn't really making money for anyone – not too good for a guy called The Moneyman!

Franny: Were you embarrassed?

Dan: A little bit. It was getting awkward in terms of my reputation as an investment expert. I was losing. I looked for good value companies which were staying good values after I bought them. Winners were soaring while losers were sinking. I wasn't out of business yet, but knew I'd be in big trouble if this lack of performance continued. Ironically, it was around this time that I appeared regularly on a TV talk show as The Moneyman. While I waited to go on a talk show one day, I experienced an epiphany of sorts that changed the way I did things.

Franny: An epiphany? Keep talking. You're waiting to go onto a

TV talk show, and you're losing money - you can't buy low and sell high anymore, right?

Dan: Right. So, I was in the television studio's Green Room waiting to go on the air. I consistently thought about the conundrum that loomed over me. I looked at the television and saw a news feed from New York. The reporter talked about a scientifically observable phenomenon concerning breast cancer surgery.

Apparently, at that time, most women with breast cancer chose the lumpectomy option over the mastectomy. Very few people were doing mastectomy anymore. Suddenly, Nancy Reagan elected to have a mastectomy. Immediately, thousands also opted to have mastectomies. Six months later, the mastectomy trend died out and lumpectomies prevailed again. While it was obvious that Nancy Reagan was getting top quality medical advice, it really made no sense for others, both breast cancer patients and surgeons, to emulate her decisions based on her unique medical history, diagnosis and situation. This was so odd, yet so typical, of the way the majority is influenced by famous people. This behavior inspired a group of university psychologists to study irrelevant celebrity endorsements and discover why people follow a prominent position, or advice, for which they know little or nothing about.

Franny: Yep, yep. I know what you mean. That sort of behavior puzzles me, too. Take Gideon, my neighbor, for instance. He loves that folk singer Tracy Chapman. He says, "If Tracy Chapman says it, I believe it!" Then, he goes and tells me I've got to watch out. The devil is everywhere in the form of people trying to sell me something, give me something and generally take me for a fool.

I tell him, "I ain't no fool." Gideon looks at me and says, "No, Franny, you're smart, that's true, but you have to look at everything inside the box, outside the box and at the lines that make the box. Like Tracy Chapman says, 'Some say the devil, he a mystical thing. I say the devil he a walking man. He a fool he a liar, conjurer and a thief. He try to tell you what you want. Try to tell you what you need.'"

Anyho, Dan The Moneyman, you are politely listening to me, although I have interrupted you. I get what you're saying about people just following celebrities like sheep. Please, go on.

Dan: Right. Say, what's your name again?

Franny: Franny, Franny Gold.

Dan: Well, Franny, it's sort of like Gideon's worship of Tracy Chapman, although in that case, he may be the only one in his crowd. I don't know. I'm not up on the folk singer movement these days.

The tendency to follow the crowd was so noticeable that a group of psychologists studied it, which led to a new concept, "information wave."

Basically, this means that in today's culture of information, the general population (or the masses) are better connected than ever – maybe better than they were meant to be! Everyone knows the same thing simultaneously. While there are many different people, they often act in unison, creating a "wave." The wave is not one of information but rather of people *reacting* to information. When I realized how cohesive public behavior was in terms of investing in the stock market, I coined the term "the herd" to describe the majority of people who respond similarly to stock market stimulus. Do you get what I'm saying, Ms. Gold? The wave is how people act as a group when they hear news about the stock market. Basically, the wave is not the market; it's the way people react to changes in the market.

Franny: I get it. I get it. I know you're making a point, but you've got to keep your head down, OK? What you're saying… It's like when everyone at a concert does the wave because the band sings a certain song.

Dan. Exactly! So, you want to know how I made my money? Well, when this total herd connection started, I lost a lot of money and didn't know why; it totally puzzled me. Here I was studying the investments, the stimulus instead of the reactor, the herd. Like when a herd of cows hears a gunshot, the early adopter cows start running. First the leaders run, followed by the entire herd. The early cows don't recall why they're running, but the herd grows larger if gunshots continue. If the gunshots stop, the cows will – one by one – start to remember that they are individuals and hungry. They will begin to move autonomously again. I compare an "information wave" to a rock thrown into a pond. Once the rock, or stock market change, is thrown into the pond, the corresponding ripples of the herd response are easy to measure. You can see how big they are and how long they might last. Until the rock hits the pond, the molecules of water move separately and are too difficult to measure. You see, the fact that they all move together makes them easy to follow.

I sat there in the Green Room, and this whole idea hit me. I said, "Holy Cow, this is my problem. I've been watching the stone trying to figure it out when I should have been watching the ripples on the pond!"

You want to know how I felt? Imagine a seventy-year-old Jew in Egypt pushing a rock to the pyramid. To the right, he sees teenagers rolling boulders on logs. "How obvious. How could I have missed that all these years?" It was my moment of revelation.

Franny: Whoa! Moment of revelation? That is *so* cool. Those moments always create a shift. A shift is actually what I need if I'm going to make more than Ivana Trump's maid gets paid. I need

a shift: a moment of revelation. Gideon has had his. He says that
it came when he heard Tracy Chapman live sing, "Let me speak
the word that precedes bliss. Love, love, love, love, love, love,
love, love." After that, Gideon's all about what he calls "awaken-
ing love." Keep going, Dan.

Dan: OK. Well, it was a shift for me. I went from looking at what
the company does, or what happens on the news, to looking at the
herd's *reaction* to them. It was a *huge* shift. I went out right away
and bought a piece of software that does a lot of back testing to
look at movements that had occurred in the past and measure the
herd reaction. This program let me try things to see if I could
begin to identify when the herd is moving in a predictable or
understandable way, and when those moves are associated with
other events and changes. I did it by trial and error; I used the
software to practice thousands of trades using historical, social
and economic events – you name it, I tried it. I did more trading
during a few months than I had in my previous forty years. I began
realizing when and why the herd formed, plus which pasture it was
likely to graze.

You see, this is really about understanding people – what they're
feeling and especially what they want. People are complicated
when they're acting as individuals; however, they're much easier
to read and measure in a cluster – just like the molecules of
water or the cows in a herd.

11

At this point in my life, I just stand on the sidelines patiently waiting for a better opportunity if I can't read the herd or know if people are caught up in the herd. The one thing I never want to do, though, is to get caught up in the herd mentality.

Franny: I'm puzzled. How could you be the only one who knows this?

Dan: All the big guys know this stuff. They might use different images or see it from different angles; regardless, they must determine what people want and help them get it. They know they have to select a different path from the crowd, so they can benefit from the crowd's movement.

I'm telling it to you because you're the only one who doesn't know it – you and everybody who just looks inside the box or outside of the box, like your friend Gideon says, and not at the lines defining the box. You think the box is reality, but it's really just drawn in there for you by the people you look to define your reality – experts, reporters, leaders, teachers. Some of them have their own agendas, you know.

Franny: Oh, now you're agreeing with Gideon? I guess you both have a point. Great session, Dan. We'll stop here, and I'll see you in two days. Thanks for sharing. I think I'm getting it. Watch those arm weights. Your triceps are pretty tender.

Points

- Contrary to popular opinion, economic and political events seldom cause stock market moves in anything but the very shortest time frame.

- People caught up in a group or a mob are much easier to understand and anticipate than the same people when they are acting as complex individuals.

- The key to making money in the stock market is understanding the mood of the herd, namely, the hunger to assume risk by buying stocks, or the intensity of the desire to reduce anxiety by selling. This is especially true when the secular trend for stock prices is sideways, as it has been for the past seven years, and as it is likely to be for the next few years, at least.

- Once you know where the herd is going, you can get there before them. You can buy what they are falling in love with and sell what they are falling out of love with.

- Avoid being fooled by what you think investors SHOULD be doing. Base your strategy on what IS.

- Remember: the best opportunities arise when the herd doesn't do what it SHOULD!

Franny's Thoughts

You wouldn't say that I have a big mouth because that implies someone who can't keep a secret. You wouldn't exactly say that I have the gift of gab either because that sort of implies that I can't shut up. My name is Francisca Adreinne D'Ore, but, like I told Dan, everyone calls me Franny: Franny Gold.

So like I was saying, I am a nimble raconteur, and I attribute my rapid rise in the bodywork industry to this ability to spin words into gold. Granted, any massage therapist has to have the fore-arms and fingers of a Clydesdale, which I do, by the way.

I work at the High Rise Houston Athletic Club. Due to my superlative combo package, I was referred by a grateful client whose neck I rearranged to be the permanent massage therapist at this posh gym/spa. I mean these guys like that I'm a woman, yet I have hands that can wring water out of sandstone. Add my virtuoso skills at extemporaneous speech, and you've got a massage therapist with medical *and* dental. Anyway, I digress.

What really interests me is how these fat cats made all their dough. Yeah, *that's* what I was thinking when I took this job. I was thinking, "I can squeeze 'em for the inside secrets."

The next day, I thought about Dan The Moneyman's advice. I must admit that I follow the crowd when it comes to investing money. About three years ago, I was dating this guy Omar from Syria.

Footnote: I don't date American men anymore because I can't afford to travel and want to see the world. When I date men from places far and wide it really is very close to being there. So far, I've seen Egypt, Syria, Iran, Germany, France, Eritrea, Japan and Kenya.

Omar was an engineer at a big telecom firm. He shows up, his eyes all bright with wealth and tells me that I should definitely put as much money as I can into this stock because it's splitting like the sands in the desert. He says all the guys at work are making millions a quarter. I don't know a DSL from a switch hitter, but I go ahead and put 10,000, my only 10,000, on that stock. Low and behold what do you know if I don't earn five in eight months and then lose twelve in three months. That's where it is now. I bought so high that I'll never make that money back. It's down the drain just like the relationship. He lost half a million and moved to San Francisco to live with relatives. He lost his house after they laid him off.

You're a herd member; I'm a herd member. I didn't share any of this information with Gideon right away. He would just gloat about Dan agreeing with his lines of the box approach. Can you be in a herd if the herd is like about not being in the herd?

Massage Session #2

Franny: (I think that guy can read my mind. When he came for his next massage, he showed me a picture of himself with long, curly hair and a big beard, wearing a cowboy hat, standing next to a wooden house built on a 1968 Chevrolet pickup.)

Dan: I laugh when I look at this picture of myself living the "alternative" lifestyle. I don't know what I was thinking at the time. It seemed like a good idea, but I simply cannot imagine why. Now it seems so totally foreign; I was just a mindless member of the herd. I guess we all looked like that back then.

Franny: Radical. Like at the club when all you guys get hair transplant plugs at the same time?

Dan: Sort of. (cough) Ms. Gold, you can't treat your money like the latest fashion or cosmetic surgery. Thinking as an individual isn't enough, since even individuals are likely to make poor decisions when the adrenaline flows. You have to force yourself to wake up and then think your situation and strategy through ahead of time. When it comes to your money, you've got to have a clear plan, not just improvise in the heat of battle.

Think about when the Allies landed on Normandy. They didn't just land and then everybody decide where they wanted to go. On the ship, the officers assembled in a safe, comfortable environment and reviewed every eventuality. They devised a plan for each possible outcome.

For you to keep *and grow* your money, you need to plan exactly what you're going to do outside of the inevitable adrenaline rush. Then I suggest that you stick with your plan no matter what! When your adrenaline is flowing, that's the time to follow your plan. You will not want to do it because you will be a part of the herd. Push back against your adrenaline and avoid following the herd! When the herd is in a panic buying mode, I am too, but I follow my written plan even when my whole body is screaming "Keep it! Keep it! It's still going up!" At the moment of truth, Ms. Gold, I honestly never feel like following my plan. Discipline alone forces me to stick with it. Meanwhile, every cell in my brain tries to seduce me into jumping on the losing train.

Here's what the very rich have always known, but nobody ever told you: The default place for your money is in your pocket, not in a diversified portfolio. This advice contradicts TV, radio and popular press.

Rich people believe that money belongs in their pocket until a compelling deal comes along. Their position goes like this, "My money belongs in my pocket, and I only commit resources when I have a specific strategy and a firm belief that I'll be well compensated for loaning my capital. If I think the deal involves substantial risk, I must be rewarded well for taking that risk! "

You see, the big guys know that DOING NOTHING IS ACTU-ALLY DOING SOMETHING. They know full well that there's never been a deal so good you can't walk away from it. Capital is rare. Offers and deals are plentiful when you have the money. Turn down one and another comes along soon enough. Regular people, on the other hand, are indoctrinated into believing that they should be in a rush to have all their assets committed all the time. They'll miss the boat if they don't hurry up and take advantage of this opportunity. Plunge.

I develop strategies that are compelling to me and that I believe are captivating with a strong likelihood of success. I measure twice and cut once, and every minute of every day, I say to myself, "I have no beliefs." There's never been a deal so good that I can't walk away from it.

Franny: So, you sort of inoculate yourself against the virus of the herd? You just repeat a mantra to yourself like "I have no beliefs" when you get that rush that tells your brain that you're going to miss out. You adhere to the plan you made, right?

Dan: Yes, and, it's not mandatory for my money to always be invested. Basically, the stock market is not creating gains right now; therefore, keep your money in your bank account until you find a compelling reason to invest it.

Franny: OK, so I have about 30,000 dollars in various mutual funds. Are you saying that I should cash those out?

Dan: Not necessarily. That's just another attempt at finding a simple answer. What I'd do is actually look carefully at each mutual fund you own. Then go to a Web site like Yahoo Finance or even – God forbid – read the quarterly report the mutual fund sends you. You'll see exactly which companies you're betting your retirement on. The simple question to ask is: Do those companies, in your mind, represent the very best way to use your scarce, hard-earned capital to help people get what they want? Because that's really what you're trying to do with your investment dollars – use them to help people get what they want *and* be compensated for it.

You want to understand my system and how people get rich, Ms. Gold? That's how. Wake up and examine your choices with a microscope rather than following the herd down the simple path to the "promised land."

Franny: That sounds like it could take a lot of time. I still spend all day trying to make a living here, you know!

Dan: Truthfully, it doesn't take any more time or trouble to do things right. Just change what goes on in your mind.

Take all the time you've spent trying to look and feel smart to the people around you and all the time you've spent watching TV and reading magazines to see what some media guy or some investment firm thinks you should do. How about taking some of the time and effort you spend maintaining your connection to that herd, to look around you and think for yourself about how to deploy your assets?

It's not about time and effort, Ms. Gold, it's about thinking like a leader instead of thinking like a follower.

Don't ignore the herd. You need to know where the herd is going, so you can travel in the opposite direction. In essence, don't be a follower.

Franny: You're starting to scare me. I mean Jeez Louise. First of all, most people feel uncomfortable standing alone. Second of all, I'm a *woman,* for God's sake! I've got what I call "the woman's disease." Naturally, I don't have it as bad as *most,* but even exceptional women have it. It's like that thing that attacks trees, oak wilt. Women are like totally brainwashed not to ever take risks with money or be leaders except when it comes to fashion, childcare and cooking or businesses *around* fashion, childcare and cooking. You're like cutting against the grain, Mr. Dan.

Dan: You're scared and that's probably because you probably haven't thought this way since you were a teenager. Actually, you've been putting yourself in *much more* danger by sleep-walking. I'm asking you to wake up! You know about lemmings, don't you? I'm sure lemmings feel very safe following along, but they don't end up very well. There's a little lemming in all of us. Sometimes the safest thing to do is what feels the most dangerous.

Franny: Like what? What could possibly be safe when it feels very dangerous?

Dan: Sometimes human nature will kill you.

I have to tell you about one of the most profound experiences and lessons of my life. I don't like to talk much about this stuff, but it has stuck with me for forty-three years.

I was a marine machine gunner in Vietnam. We would be at-tached to rifle platoons in the Pacific. So you get trained for an ambush where the enemy knows you're coming and he's ready. He's got the escape routes covered.

So you get into this spot, and the ambush opens up on you. First, you freeze with fear. The human herd instinct is to run away, but if you do, you'll get cut down like a stick of butter.

There's really only one thing to do, and you may get killed by doing it, but you're definitely getting killed if you don't.

You have to rush the strongest part of the ambush head on. You know you'll lose a lot of guys, maybe all of them, but you're a dead man anyway.

You rush the strongest point, and if some of you get through, you live. Boy, this is the exact opposite of human nature. What could be more pathetic than to watch a herd of guys, blindly running away, getting cut down, without a chance?

Where's the analogy? I guess it is that you must go against your nature to survive sometimes. In the Marines, they drill you on it over and over and over, until it's part of you. Even at sixty, I still attack automatically if I feel cornered. It's that much a part of you.

For the past few years, I've had seventy percent of my money in safe investments. I didn't have that ten or even eight years ago. I saw it was going to get harder than ever, so I decided to go for bonds. It sounds risky to move away from investing in the stock market. Moving away from investing in the stock market is definitely going against the herd.

Here's what I get for opting out, though:

In the next year or two – late 2006 or 2007 – I'm looking forward to the best buying opportunity of the decade. I'm planning to have most of my money in the stock market by mid-2007 at the latest, and I expect to be buying stocks at much lower prices than those that exist today. The great thing is I'll have plenty of money to buy with because of not losing a lot of money in a falling stock market. I've had positive returns in horrible years, better performance in the stock market because of less fear, and I've been able to be much more selective about where and when I take risk.

To take risk, I've been able to demand much better than nine or ten percent a year. If it's only a little better, why should I take the risk? I'm already making good money without it. You want low risk? Move away from your comfort zone. Wake up! I think you'll actually have more fun and feel much safer in the end.

Franny: So, you are actually an Ex-Marine? I was just thinking, "What a gentle soul." Goes to show you, even a Marine machine gunner can have a gentle personality.

Gideon is helping me understand war. At its root, of course, it's greed. We've agreed on that, but then there are elements of needing to feel powerful and also of creating identity. I mean, personally, I think art does those things without the loss of life, but what do I know? Sorry, I digress. The whole analogy derailed me.

OK. When I encounter resistance to telling my broker to move my money around in ways that he didn't initiate, I need to think about it with the same guts and independence that I had when I sold the new Ethan Allen couch my mother gave me for Christmas on the front lawn and used the money to go to Bali. Is that basically it?

Dan: Yes, it's about being you and not someone else. Find that core individualism. Not to get too philosophical, but over my sixty years, I've become convinced that a big part of our lives as human beings is about moving back and forth between being an intelligent individual and a mindless herd animal.

I actually force myself to *wake up* every day because it's easy to be like everybody else. Over time, I do feel less and less resistance to following my plan, though. Just like those fingers of yours got stronger and stronger the more you used them, so does the part of your brain that thinks like a leader the more you use it.

I hope you're starting to get that making money during these times is more a function of psychology than it is of math. Human beings are herd animals. We have noticed, as I'm sure you have, that smart people are often "dumbed down" when they act as part of a group, mob or herd. Think of the townspeople in a movie where they form a lynch mob. Remember most of them are law-abiding citizens.

When a group mentality sets in, human beings tend to move with it. It takes courage to stand back.

I recently heard about a man in London who became enraged at a soccer match and kicked a man in the head, killing him. He is an intelligent man but as he became a part of the herd, his IQ declined rapidly. He woke up in jail after being an accountant for fifteen years with a wife and kids and sitting on the board at his kids' school. Now, he's in jail for murder. He's asking himself, "How could I have done this? What was I thinking?"

It happened because there are actually two totally different people inside him, a sensitive, decent citizen and a mindless herd animal. As the individual, he can't imagine how he could have done anything so disgusting, but when he was caught up in that group-think, that violent acting out seemed like a good idea!

I think about that silly picture of me from the sixties, and I realize it's only by sheer dumb luck or the grace of God that I didn't do something much worse and get myself in real trouble. What makes this so insidious is that when you are captivated or hypnotized by the herd, you don't know it. We all tend to rationalize and convince ourselves that we are not falling in line with the mass psychology of the moment but are, in fact, making wise, astute choices. We do this when nothing could be farther from the truth. The truth is we're like the man who meets a pretty girl and instead of thinking about having sex with her, he's thinking about what his friends will think of her. Is that why you're in the market, to look good in front of your friends, your broker and your wife?

If you remember nothing else, remember this: If you are actually investing in the stock market to *make money*, then you must learn how to *identify herd behavior,* and you must learn how to *prevent yourself from becoming a member of the herd*. You're going to have to identify your own herd behavior and stop it. The most important thing to keep in mind is we're trying to help people get what they want. We're thinking about other people. When you're swept up in the herd, you're only thinking about yourself, what you want, what people think about you. That is not how you get rich, Ms. Gold. There is only one reason to have a herd and that is for slaughter. Your job is to stay awake and think about how to help people get what they want.

Franny: That's a wrap for today, Dan. We went a little over, but that's OK. My next guy cancelled anyway. You've given me a lot to think about.

Dan: Thank you, that was great despite the agony. I'll see you next week, and we can talk some more.

Franny: Sounds like a plan, Dan.

Points

- Don't believe the old wives' tale that the more risk you take, the more profit you make. The real saying should be, "The more risk you take, the more profit you can make, and the more likely you are to lose."

- Make an overall investment plan, and make a clear plan for each individual transaction. Then stick with your plan.

- You don't always have to rely on the stock market for your investments. Like the super-rich do, only go for good deals. Sometimes that means stocks, sometimes bonds, sometimes cash, money market, foreign bonds or even private deals.

- DOING NOTHING IS ACTUALLY DOING SOME-THING. Holding out for an easy opportunity is the favorite strategy of the world's most successful investors.

- The hard part is getting the investment capital in the first place. Once you have it, be confident that there is always another good deal on the way. Make peace with the fact that you are never under pressure to hurry up and act.

- Also make peace with the fact that others will make money on things you miss. Don't run after investments you have missed. Others may be willing to take more risk, or they may simply have figured out a good plan early. Don't try to make up for your initial failure by jumping on the bandwagon late and compounding it.

- Don't confuse seeking comfort with smart investing or even safe investing. If you want comfort, take Valium. The investment world is full of uncertainty. Deal with it or don't, but don't kid yourself.

- Research each mutual fund you own on financial Web sites like Yahoo Finance or by reading the quarterly report from the fund. Ask yourself, "Do the companies in this fund represent the best way to help other people get what they want?" If the answer is yes, congratulations. If no, make the changes to bring your portfolio into line with reality.

- When the time comes to act according to your plan, expect to feel afraid to follow it. This is because your planned action will probably be very different from what the herd is doing. Be conscious of the fact that you're a member of the herd, and resist your herd impulse.

- Remember that the adrenaline rush of herd mentality makes even the most sensible people lose their minds. You're not alone, you're not an idiot, you're just a normal human being who got caught up in a group frenzy and lost money.

- Stay with the fear, and it will turn to excitement.

Franny's Thoughts

This whole thing about moving into the opposite of your feeling, it's kind of got a spiritual element to it. I mean when you look at martial arts, that's all about changing your initial desire to use force to avoiding violence.

Then, when you look at love and marriage and commitment and kids and that whole package, the only thing that's really natural about it is the sex. The rest of it, sticking with someone over time while you both get double chins and start making the same facial expressions – that's not really natural. Being nice to kids overall isn't natural either. I mean, it takes massive training to learn to just let them become who they are and to listen to them and not to whack them around. I mean, seriously, didn't people just start treating kids like human beings about twenty-five years ago?

All I'm saying is this whole move into the danger zone may not be quite as unique as Dan The Moneyman makes it out to be, maybe in terms of investment.

Anyho, I actually got a flat tire, and I was out in front of my house pumping the jack up and down underneath the bumper when Gideon came out in his front yard with three people who were obviously his mom, dad and brother. Now I know he's not adopted. They all look a little bit like Tony Danza except the mom, who looks like Danny Thomas. The whole clan comes over and Gideon says, "Franny, what are you doing?"

I'm like, "I'm getting ready to change my tire." There's this sort of group snort and then they just move in and change the tire for me. Apparently, you don't actually pump a jack, and it doesn't go under the bumper.

I met his family. They seem very nice, although a little *ou la la*, a little Malibu/Hartford, Connecticutty, if you know what I mean. There were signs of sizable incomes, which working-class people like me are brainwashed to be suspicious of. Rich people are part of the "them" that make life hard for the rest of us. At least that's the line we get growing up.

Working at The Club, I've come to realize that rich people are just like the rest of us – they just have more money. Well, that's a joke, of course, but they're actually a little bit happier, confident and more intolerant of poor people, which is just natural if you think that your affluence has something to do with you being a little bit better. It's no matter to me. To me, Franny Gold, it's all a play, something to watch and enjoy. Who knows what I'll be like when I'm rolling in dough?

One thing about men that you have to watch out for, in terms of those who can and those who cannot actually make a commitment to a significant other, is the ones who have rich and powerful fathers. These guys are a real twist. Usually I'd say that if you find yourself with what I call a "Dynasty Son" just walk away. Either they're stuffed into the old man's mold, which is a time bomb, or they're traipsing about the globe being Peter Pan with a gift for poetry, political activism or just being plain charming for as long as it lasts, i.e., until you throw them out. Talk about human nature killing you: "Stay for the charm, and you'll be harmed." That's a little motto I came up with.

When I realized that Gideon might be a Dynasty Son, I stopped having all those conversations with him in my head. It's hard, but sometimes, like Dan says, *the biggest danger is in following your natural instincts rather than your trained reason.*

When it comes to finding a long-term enduring relationship, I'm like a Green Beret on a stealth mission. My body and mind are one self-disciplined machine. Jeez! There I go with war metaphors. Next, I'll probably start liking Fox News.

Massage Session #3

Franny: Hello. You're right on time. You know the drill. I'll see you in a few minutes.

Dan: Sounds good.

Franny: How's your neck doing today? You got away from the computer, I hope.

Dan: Oh, yeah. It's doing great today. I actually took a trip out to Phoenix since I saw you last. I'm investigating a company that I'm considering investing in. It's more effort than just reading about them, but I really get to see for myself what the operation is like. They are a metallurgy company and combine different alloys to make super strong or flexible metals.

Franny: Radical. What a good idea. So, last time we were talking about using independent reasoning, moving away from the herd.

Dan: Yes, we were. As I was coming over here, I thought about golf. When you play golf, you're right out there for the world to see. It's not like you're surrounded by a jungle. A golf green is like a giant open stage where everyone can see everything you do. It's the perfect place for people to be deep in herd mentality and not know it. You hear a guy at the golf course talking about how he's making a fortune on a cancer-curing stock. Without planning, scrutiny or reflection, you decide to invest in the same stock. What goes through your head at the time is, "Oh, my god, I'm going to miss this." Then you start to imagine how smart everybody's going to think you are as all that free money starts pouring into your pocket.

Actually spending some time researching the company, its financing, what kind of competition it faces, its projections etc., is to your advantage. How many people have already invested in that stock? How much of the company are you actually getting for your hard-earned cash? It never even crosses most people's minds once they're caught up in that kind of group-think.

What happens? You lose seventy percent of your investment. You lost seventy percent because you didn't want to be embarrassed in front of your wife when the stock prices started to fall. When you started to lose, you didn't want to admit that you had no idea what you were doing. Actually helping to find a cure for a hor-rible disease wasn't even on your mind.

When you are acting as an individual and not part of the herd, it seems obvious to you that you're in the stock market to make money and help people get what they want, *not* to impress your broker or your wife and friends.

When you're on the golf course, you are often acting as part of the herd. Most of the time, we (myself included) merge into whatever beliefs and actions flow around us. This flow is the herd mentality. Your herd mentality is your evil twin, and you have to do everything in your power to move away from it. Start out like I did and for five minutes a week or more stand as an individual investor with your wits about you. Gradually, train yourself to think autonomously for longer periods of time.

Franny: Train myself to think autonomously? I like that. That's very empowering as a woman. While I don't play golf, I get your analogy. It's like when I was dating Daichi, the Japanese guy, and I told my girlfriends that he had taken me out for a salad on my birthday. Jeez Louise, it was like the howl of the Amazonians, "Get rid of him!" Women can be so intolerant. Why not give the guy another chance? You know, wait until Valentine's Day and see what happens. It got so bad among the girlfriends that I actually kept the fact that I was still seeing him a secret. Standing autonomously is harder than it looks.

Then when Omar (the boyfriend before Daichi) told me to buy and everyone was buying, I remember feeling like someone else was running my brain. I just had to have it right away. It would be so horrible for me to miss out! I just had to hurry up. The train was leaving the station without me. I was like, "Just get me in at any price!" As it turned out, Daichi brought me an orchid and took me out for my favorite food, French, on Valentine's Day. He was very good about eating snails, too.

Dan: Exactly, Ms. Gold. You were the one in the relationship, not them. The truth is that when all is said and done, you are the one who wakes up alone in the morning knowing that you've lost seventy percent of your money or in your case, a man named Daichi. All those people who said, "This is the way to go," where are they? You ask yourself, "How could I have done this?" Like the guy who murdered someone at a soccer game; he "woke up" and looked at what he had done with horror, thinking, "What do I care who wins a soccer game? My life is about my family, not soccer. Now, I'll sit in jail for twenty years." Your life would be far better if you never invested another penny in the stock market than if you simply follow the current trends and refuse to admit that you're wrong when you make a mistake.

Franny: I'm a little freaked out by what you're saying, I have to admit. My guy that manages my money says that I can earn six or seven percent a year on the stock market. Isn't that good, or does it even keep up with inflation? He's a very sweet man. I don't think he would knowingly take me for a ride.

Dan: Are you investing in those mutual funds because you researched them and you feel like those particular companies contribute to the world in the way that you want to contribute? Or are you investing in those mutual funds because everyone does and you feel uncomfortable doing something different? You said you don't play golf, right?

Franny: No, I sea-kayak.

Dan: Well, in golf, there's an old pro named Chi Chi Rodriguez. Chi Chi Rodriguez has always played golf professionally. He told me that when he played privately for money, he would always watch how the other player acted when that player was about to take a swing. If the other player looked up to see who was watching, Chi Chi knew that that guy was a loser. At the top level of any game, including investing, you are doing it for yourself and nobody else...or you lose.

A lot of people make a mistake and then they don't want to admit it to themselves or to the people they feel compelled to impress, so they stay on the wrong course. You see this on the golf course a lot. Someone makes a mistake and hits the ball into the trees. He hangs onto a macho illusion and doesn't want to lose the stroke, so he looks for a way to go directly from the trees to the green. He gets sucked into trying an even harder shot through the trees, and he often ends up ruining the whole day with a twelve. Sometimes it just takes one ego-driven mistake, and your game is over, Ms. Gold. And you know, I suspect women are mostly immune to this sports machismo thing, but they're just as worried about impressing their friends in other ways.

Referring back to my male example: A top player hits a ball into the trees looking for the best route out to the green to recover his play. Usually that means accepting the fact that his bad shot cost him a stroke. So he takes an easy shot onto the fairway, and the next shot puts him right on the green where he wants it. The pros don't waste time avoiding the fact that they hit the ball into the trees in the first place! When they hit the inevitable bad shot, they're at peace with the fact that it costs them a stroke on the scorecard.

If they are honest, many people will actually wonder what their stock broker, or their friends, or their wife *will think of them* when they make a mistake in the market. If the investor is a man, and a woman is watching, he will likely pay to be right. I mean he'll fight to stay in denial. He'll refuse to change course and admit his error.

Golf and investing aren't like tennis or football; adrenaline doesn't help in golf or investing. The smallest error can screw the deal up. That's why you can't be a winner at golf if you're worried about what other people think. You can only be a winner if you stand apart from the herd, focus on your game, and play it for yourself and nobody else. Investing is just like that. The game is using your capital to help people get what they want. It's when you get caught up in fear about love, self-worth and all that psychobabble that you start to run on adrenaline. It's the kiss of death for an investor.

Franny: I hear you on that! I know every time I bring home an Arab or an African, my mother says, "What will people think?" I mean, who cares? This is my life philosophy: *Get over it.*

I can admit I'm wrong; though, I've noticed that Gideon can't. Last night we were talking about blood – he's in charge of the blood bank – and he spouts off all of these facts about blood like fifty pints of blood is six times the amount a human being holds in his body, and the binding of hemoglobin to something causes something. I don't know. I told him that a lot of recipes call for cooking the meat in its own blood, like rabbit, for instance.

He just stares at me and says, "That's not true." Well, of course it's true, and I have a cookbook to prove it. I got it out and showed it to him, *Le lapin dans le jus de viande de sang*. Not once did he admit that he was wrong. He will go on denying the reality of blood-gravy recipes just to be right. I swear he will. He says to me, "Franny, where are you from?" He says it in a way that implies that I am from Mars. I said, "I'm from a little-known region of Pennsylvania. Where are you from?"

Turns out, Gideon *is* from another country, Malibu. Once I realized that he came from the land of movie stars, I found him even more confusing: his need to be a Tracy Chapman groupie, his adoration of Magic Johnson, his interest in meditation. He explained it to me, though. He says that he's just sick of the blond aesthetic and all it represents.

Franny's Thoughts

(Between you and me, I'm a blue-eyed blonde, a fact I consider to be unfortunate in today's world, especially working at the Houston High Rise Club, where that's like a ticket to ride. The last thing I wanted to do is cash in on my looks. My skill at the table and my great conversation are enough. I wear green contacts, and most people know me as a redhead. There are those who would argue for self-acceptance and others who would stand for imaginative costuming. I'm with both groups. A little voice in my brain wonders if I should ever tell Gideon the truth since he has such a thing about the blond aesthetic.)

(I'm starting to think that Gideon might not have the terrible Dynasty Son Syndrome. Although it's possible. I mean he *seems* balanced. It's not across the board; the Dynasty Son Syndrome thing, I mean. From time to time, there is a rich, powerful father who doesn't wear his influence like a suit of armor. Occasionally, you find love, tenderness and non-arrogance. OK, I admit, I've never actually found it, but in theory, I believe in it. So if Gideon really is a down-to-earth Dynasty Son who can hold his own identity and a job at the same time, it's a *miracle*.)

Points

- The desire to impress your friends, please your spouse or even your financial advisor is your herd mentality in action. Learn to recognize it.

- Notice how often you consider what others may say or think about you when you consider making a move to follow your investment plan. Notice the same thing in other facets of your life as well. When you catch yourself doing this, simply wake up!

- The best example of what it feels like to follow the herd is when you "pay to be right." In other words, you're willing to lose money rather than admit you made a mistake and take a loss.

- Be willing to accept large gains, small gains and small losses. Do not let a small loss turn into a large one because you are "paying to be right!"

Massage #3 continued

Franny: Anyho, Dan, I do understand what you're saying. You're saying that people will just watch their money dwindle away in investments that they know almost nothing about just to avoid admitting that they didn't know what the hell they were doing in the first place. Is that right?

Dan: Yes, as long as they're going to invest according to what everyone else is doing and refuse to admit they are wrong, they're not going to make much, if any, money. If you think about it logically, you don't have to be an expert on everything; you don't have to know what all the Wall Street jargon means. You really only have to find a few ways to use your capital to help people get what they want, and here's the next lesson: You have to *stay awake and make sure you're getting a good deal on the investment itself.* Some companies offer a good deal for the investors while others use a great story to get people excited; in the end, both give investors very little for their money. If you don't get a good deal, you will lose money on even the coolest idea.

That's the game on Wall Street. They suck people in with a good story, and the patsies end up with nothing, Ms. Gold. Do you know what happens when a person with money meets a person with experience?

Franny: I know you're going to tell me!

Dan: THE PERSON WITH THE EXPERIENCE ENDS UP WITH THE MONEY, AND THE PERSON WITH THE MONEY ENDS UP WITH EXPERIENCE.

You can use all that free information when it comes to understanding the actual companies – how they handle money and whether they offer a good deal. Most big-time pros do their own objective accounting stuff; however, there's plenty of great company research available for a small amount of money. You can even go to the library and read about thousands of companies in *Valueline* or *Standard and Poors*. These services are great at analyzing the companies and their values. Unfortunately, that public information is useless unless you know *what* people want and *when* they want it. Those services and the free information on the Internet won't tell you that.

Now here's the secret that pulls it all together: The way you get a good deal on a good idea that everybody knows about is to catch the herd when it is running the wrong way.

Franny: Oh, that's what you meant earlier by continuing to monitor the herd's activities but not to follow it, right?

Dan: Right! Remember: when you know what everyone else knows, you know nothing. By the time you know about something, everyone else does, too. So the trick isn't to be the only one who knows about something. That's just not going to happen very often. You're playing in the big leagues.

So I know which investments I want to make, and then I wait for millions of regular investors to get swept up in some kind of stampede. I don't want to compete against smart, educated professionals who have all the inside information, all the tools and all the money in the world. I want to compete against a herd of cows. I only get involved when I see the herd moving in the wrong direction. It's like taking candy from a baby!

Franny: I have to say, Dan, that's sort of Machiavellian.

Dan: Remember, Ms. Gold: although money by itself won't make you happy, you can sure use it to make a lot of other people happy. If you mean it's calculated, you're right. If you mean I organize events to create a good outcome for myself, right again. In martial arts, you use your opponent's force against him. It's the same idea. You're using the force of the stampede for your own benefit.

When you can't tell what the herd is doing and some "expert" is pointing to the price to earning (P/E) ratio saying the stock is undervalued, stop and think! Ask yourself, "If we figured this out, what makes me think that people with more inside information haven't figured it out, also?" This game is not about making the news and foretelling the future. Why? Because you don't have as good information as the insiders and you can't foretell the future. They *are* the market, so they know what everybody's buying and selling. These guys are seeing the orders and can see what's happening in real time. You don't know any of it.

Franny: Like when I watch the Discovery channel and I find out that a plant nursery in Cameroon, Africa, is growing a rare plant that cures AIDS, I shouldn't invest in it because the big guys are way ahead of me on that?

Dan: Umm...not exactly. Nothing attracts bad deals like a good story. The question here – for me – would be, how much of the company and its profits are you selling to me for my 20,000? What percentage do I own? I'd rather have a good deal on a less glamorous story than a lousy deal on a company with the greatest invention of the century.

Also, it's more like if you watch CNN or CNBC and some pundit recommends buying or selling. If buying is such a good idea, the big guys have already done it. If you do it after watching that show, you will be one of millions. How much money do you think you're going to make when the market is glutted with members of the herd all going after the same stocks? Not much.

Number one, you don't know what the P/E ratio is because that accounting, which is often wrong, is done to promote a certain story. Most companies actually keep at least two sets of books: One for reporting to the public and for tax rules and another for management to have a view of the big picture.

Number two, P/E ratio is total bullshit. The past is over, and these guys have shown no ability to even forecast what they'll be eating for lunch next week. So the average Joe thinks he's being rigorous by comparing P/E ratios, but he's only comparing the emotional assessments of the managers. If they were good at forecasting, they wouldn't be getting divorced or fired every other year. For instance, when you come to the conclusion that stock XYZ will be a great investment because next July they will be approved by the FDA for their cure for diabetes or you're going to buy the stock because it's undervalued, then I suggest that you sound an alarm. Sound the "herd alarm." You are acting like the herd. Hopefully, you will have programmed yourself to recognize this and step away from taking any action.

There is a seventy-five percent chance that you think it's undervalued because you heard it said on TV. This is herd behavior and *herd behavior equals slaughter*. If the stock really is undervalued, then much smarter people knew this before you. Accept the fact that you don't have the information, experience or staying power to win. Why do you think they have to do the tests and trials on drugs in the first place? If they knew how the trials were going to come out, why would most of the tests fail? Do you know how much money it costs to conduct clinical testing on new drugs?

You may be wise to invest in the plant in Cameroon. Just really think the deal through as if someone actually knocked on your door and personally asked you to invest in his business.

But that's still a private deal. It's off the beaten track, and it's a little different from the kind of investing most people do in the stock market. In the public market, everybody pretty much knows the same facts about the same companies. The only way you get a good deal on a company is to catch the herd when it is worried and pessimistic – buy the stock when most inexperienced investors want to sell in fear.

Likewise, when the herd is feeling very optimistic and exhilarated, you should think about selling your stock to them. They'll be happy to pay you way too much for it.

Matter-of-fact, this is so important. I hope we get a chance to really talk about it sometime. For now, let's just agree that you don't behave like a mindless robot in your normal day to day life or you wouldn't be here in good health, making a decent living.

Franny: Yeah. I lost money on that high-tech stock because I just went with the flow. Sometimes I'm just a wuss.

48

Dan: We all are. That's why we have to have a plan and stick with it. March of 2000 was a time when a lot of people found out they didn't know as much as they thought. They bought into the story that there was a technology boom all around the world. They said to themselves, "It has got to keep going forever, so it's safe for me to stay on course with these high-tech investments." It was like a group-think mantra. I got caught up in it myself.

The truth wasn't too hard to see because it happens repeatedly. When you have something that's very profitable, it attracts competition. Investors are dying to put their capital to work, which helps people get what they want.

When barriers to entry are low, it attracts competition. In the late nineties, technology continued to spread and tons of capital poured into the high-tech market.

No longer were investors using their capital to help people get what they wanted. They were latecomers to the party and focused on collecting easy money – getting something for nothing.

Eventually, nobody was left to buy those stocks. Everyone agreed on how great they were and had already invested as much as they could. With a little push from the Fed, the buying stopped. Without demand, the stock prices fell and people started losing money. As an individual, you might have said to yourself, "My God, it took me my entire life to earn this money.

I see the character of the market has changed, so I have to stop risking all my money on this one sector."

You also might have said, "These high-tech companies like Microsoft have all the capital they could ever use. How can I expect the world to reward me for throwing more capital at them? All I'm doing is gambling. I'm buying paper in the hopes of selling it to somebody else at a higher price."

As a member of the herd, however, most people were sold on the idea of making a killing in high-tech; they considered themselves bulletproof and forgot the whole point of investing in the stock market.

Franny: To help people get what they want, right?

Dan: Right. Instead of selling out when the character of the market changed, each member of the herd listened to his broker, who didn't know a thing himself! By the time most investors realized the change was real, they became the guy looking around on the putting green. They were more worried about what their wives and friends thought than winning the game.

Once the herd mentality took over, the losing investors became more afraid of humiliation than losing money. They were afraid that as soon as they sold, the stock prices would go up.

An investor who had strategically chosen to be over-committed to certain stocks because he saw a special opportunity, thinking as an individual with any semblance of common sense, would surely lighten up with the first inkling that the market was changing. In the late nineties, so many people were so caught up in the herd that they didn't care. These were smart people who had been successful in business and should have known better. They watched seventy percent of their money disappear and as it was going away, at no time did they stop it. Since they had enough to eat today, their number one concern was how others thought of them. They forgot about the principle of using capital to help people get what they want. Their overriding concern was the love and respect of their fellow herd members.

Franny: I could be sea-kayaking in New Zealand right now if I hadn't thrown my money into the group pot. I guess those heavy hitters you're talking about came out clean?

Dan: Yep. After the bear market was over, I took a look at the balance sheets of Merrill Lynch. The customers' net worth had fallen by forty to seventy percent, but *the net worth of the investment house was higher*! Why? It was higher because they sold their stocks and moved into bonds. The big guys weren't acting as part of the herd. And most importantly, they weren't doing what they told their customers to do. The big guys knew what they were doing and they knew when to do it. You can never know as much as they do, but you *can* learn how to invest as an individual and *resist* the call of the herd.

Franny: We're done for today, Dan The Moneyman. I would like to hear what you have to say about how I can avoid all these psychological pitfalls and actually make money. Save up your wisdom for next time. I'm suggesting these three yoga moves for your lower back. Go practice them in the outer room, and I'll see you next Tuesday!

Before you go…You know, Dan, I have a funny feeling. I think I'm shifting. I might be approaching a moment of revelation. Do you ever realize that suddenly you have a lot of suppressed dreams? I would love to go to Spain and see the Gaudi buildings. He's an architect. I *love* Gaudi. I call him "the insect man" because his buildings look like the creations of insects: very perfect and non-human. I don't think dating a Spaniard will give me the same thrill as being inside of one of Gaudi's creations. There are other things, too. I'd like to write a book for men about how to choose a good woman, not just a pretty one. I've seen a lot of things working here with these guys. Anyho, all this takes dough, and I'm realizing that I really want to create what Gideon calls "a passive income stream."

Dan: There's really nothing passive about it. You have to keep yourself awake and in charge. See you next time!

Points

- Know which investments are made as real commitments to specific companies and which are trades based on the herd. These two strategies are not the same and should never be confused.

- Take the time to learn the real story about or even actually go visit companies you are interested in making a real commitment to. Also, take the trouble to understand the companies' finances.

- Use research services to obtain inexpensive financial information on companies. Use the Internet, go to the library, and read *Valueline* and *Standard and Poors*.

- Remember, some companies offer a good deal for the investors while others use a great story to get people excited. A great story is often the best way to a bad deal. Stay awake.

- When you know what everyone else knows, you know nothing. If the expert on TV is telling a story about a company and the herd is acting on it, the trade is over. This is one of those times to be at peace with the fact that you can't be in on every deal.

- If you love the story and believe in the company, wait. Catch the herd when it is worried and pessimistic – buy the stock when most inexperienced investors want to sell in fear.

- When the herd is feeling very optimistic and exhilarated, you should think about selling your stock to them. They'll be happy to pay you way too much for it.

- Forecasts and P/E ratios are of limited use. They can tell you what SHOULD be happening. The most profitable piece of knowledge you will ever get is the knowledge that what SHOULD happen often DOESN'T!

- Recognize TV pundits for what they are – the leaders of the herd.

- Think through each specific commitment to a company as if someone personally came to your house and asked you to invest your money in their private business. This is a more familiar situation than the stock market for many people, and they are often more adept at navigating it.

- Make sure your strategic plan includes the knowledge that the economy is always moving through its cycles and is always changing. Be ready. Remember: the stock market has been very sensitive to changes in the economy since year 2000, and a bad stock market will often demolish the stocks of perfectly good companies.

- Don't let concern about what other people will think about you be more important to you than the primary purpose of stock market investing – helping people get what they want. If you focus on using your capital to bring goods and services to people who want them, you will make money. If you focus on looking smart to your group, you will lose money.

Franny and Gideon

Franny: Gideon stopped by Saturday to ask me how my tire was doing. I told him it was doing just fine. I chit-chatted around and hit upon how nice it was to meet his family. "So what sort of work do your parents do?" I asked him.

His parents own a chain of sperm labs, it turns out. They cater to the whole fertility market and run all of the DNA and disease tests. They're certified in some way, he says. That explains his interest in blood. As a matter of fact, it turns out that he's actually part owner of the blood bank where he works.

When you're dealing with a Dynasty Son, there is a certain way to find out whether he's split from the mother/father ship enough to fly on his own. First, you let him chatter on for about ten minutes. Lull him with gentle encouragement and interest until he's just telling you what comes to his mind without censoring it first. Then, in the space of those ten minutes, the word "mother" or "father" will come up if he has not split from the paternals. This is foolproof. When you hear it, just realize that it's over and walk away. As Dan says, "stick to your plan" and say to yourself, "I have no beliefs" unless you're like one of those females who wants a long-term enduring relationship with a bank account, then go right ahead.

Of course, you can go on and ask him what his father does, but it's really not necessary. For instance, I once went out with a Dynasty Son (one of several) whose father competed in the Olympics. Now, this fellow chose the Peter Pan route. He was a charmer with a string of ex-girlfriends about twenty years his junior. The real telling factor, though, was his marginal/passive-aggressive lifestyle. He was forty, working as a part-time personal trainer and going to a lot of parties where everyone wore their pajamas, which was fun in college.

The other kind are those who never left the train station. They're usually married or between marriages. They drink a lot, rely heavily on their wealth as a personality and are generally incredibly boring.

I have to tell you that Gideon does not strike me as either of these. First of all, he actually owns a business and works every day. Second, it's not his father's business. Third, he never used a sentence with the words "my mother" or "my father" in them to me. I'm going to relax about it.

I told him about the whole herd thing: watch 'em, work 'em, and move away from 'em. He listened to me and got real serious. Then he says, "I need to make a call" and takes off like a house on fire.

Sounds like I got to him in the nick of time.

He came sauntering back about an hour later with a glass of pear sake for me to try.

"So," Gideon says, giving me the shiny big eye, "did I pass?"

I just gave him a blank stare. "I have no idea what you're talking about." Then he starts in with a Tracy Chapman lyric, "We need to make new symbols/Make new signs/Make a new language/ With these we'll define the world/And start all over/Start all over/Start all over/Start all over ..."

"You can sing all the Tracy Chapman you want. I still have no idea what you're talking about."

Then we just sat in silence and drank our sake.

Massage Session #4

Franny: Hi there, Dan The Moneyman. Do you want a hot towel today? How's that lower back?

Dan: Yes on the towel, and my back is much better, thanks.

Franny: OK. I'll get that going. You remember where we left off? You were going to tell me how to invest for myself. Don't forget!

Dan: Right. I remember.

(Five minutes later)

Franny: Let's start on your biceps today. So…you were saying about my personal investment plan?

Dan: The thing is, Ms. Gold, there are actually two alternatives here: One is to invest in and commit to things you actually know everything about that would be reasonable to stay with through thick and thin – like my radio company is for me and your massage therapy career is to you. We don't quit just because we had a slow day or even because we make mistakes.

In the market, I don't have that kind of commitment. I'm speculating, and it is all about buying pieces of paper – stocks in companies. It comes down to guessing what other investors will be doing. Even then, you can have a fairly comprehensive plan.

Franny: So…like what? Give me an example. I need pictures.

Dan: OK. Here's an example of my current plan. It builds on the strategies that the Chinese have for development in China.

Right now, there is a new, five-year plan on the drawing board for China.

This is the eleventh five-year plan of the Chinese Republic, and they have huge goals. The first wave of Chinese development was all about the top three cities – Shanghai, Beijing and Shenzhen. This development has created more demand than you've ever seen. It's the development of the West times ten.

In the second wave, they're going to do a bunch of their second-tier cities inside China. If you want an idea of the scale they operate on, there are more cranes in Shanghai than in the entire United States combined. Twenty million people: that's just one big city, and get this, Chong Quing is considered a second-tier city. It has thirty-one million people!

They're going to spend four trillion dollars on this, and it's going to be forty percent more money than they spent last time, which is only the beginning. Then they'll work on the third-tier cities and spend a few trillion more.

And when they do this, they will need zinc, copper, nickel and iron ore for all that construction. So where do they get it all? From the same place you hope to get yours. Only they want theirs more, and they're willing to sacrifice more to get it!

So does the earth have enough nickel and iron? Who knows?

Nobody you know, that's for sure. But here's what I do know: It's harder to develop those resources now because you have all kinds of global warming – Kyoto, Green Day, permitting red tape, political hassles. See, you have global demands, but no global government to iron them out.

Do we want a global government? I don't.

Is it our job to put together systems so countries can produce agreements to get all these resources? Not really. If you want to help, run for Congress. You can do it, but my interest is in giving my family and your family a better life.

I'll be there to buy when the worries about the slowing economy make the prices of miners, processors and transporters of copper, iron, nickel and even oil companies drop. When a civilization is just industrializing, their use of metals per person grows very fast, and it depends on the growth of the economy.

The change in gross national product leads to a larger change in how much metals they will use – much larger than in a more industrial place like the United States. The upside surprise in the growth in China – and India, by the way – leads to a bigger up-swing in how much metals they use.

Ultimately, the surprise strength in China is much more important than the lousy performance in Europe.

As the sun sets on our tour of enchantment in the mansions overlooking the Pacific Ocean in Acapulco, we will offer a little thanks to the panicky investors, who act on their emotions, follow the herd, and buy at the top when they're confident – only to sell at the bottom when they're scared.

China's Share of World Consumption

Metal	199-LA	200-LA
Aluminum	6%	21%
Copper	7%	20%
Zinc	11%	25%
Iron Ore*	29%	36%

*Iron ore data compares 1996 and 2004

Source: AME WBMS and Goldman Sacks Research estimates.

Franny: Wow! I feel as if I just finished watching *Gone with the Wind*. Drama! That's how to have fun with your money six different ways. You figured all that out just by watching and listening didn't you? It all boils down to powers of observation.

Dan: Now you want to be a market observer, but you're not sure what to observe? Earlier in the summer, remember, we had all that talk about how surprisingly strong earnings were? Remember that? So after all that happy news, prices of stocks barely moved. The herd is no longer sensitive to happy news – that's what I get out of it. Now we will start to hear about weaker news. Weaker than expected durable goods orders! Housing slowing. Retail sales hurt. Right now the S&P is at the highs of March. How worried should you be about this slowdown – rising rates – high energy prices?

With all due respect to my friends who don't agree with me, the poor people – the ones at the bottom rung – are being affected by gasoline. Soon, they will be dealing with heating oil. Remember: They can drive less, but they really can't stop heating their houses without some real emotional pain.

Franny: Are you predicting something?

Dan: I'm observing the rest of the world. Do you realize that China recently passed privatization so people can own homes?

You want to talk about a boom! Twenty-one million people a year are moving to the city in China. People coming to the cities from the farms are filling up three New York cities every year. In the next ten years, it's going to be another 200 million people. In the next ten years, the Chinese are going to create and build something from scratch that will surpass New York City, L.A., Chicago, Dallas, Houston, Miami, Atlanta, St. Louis, Kansas City, San Francisco – all the big cities in the United States, and these will be built from the ground up.

Franny: It's hard to imagine. And these people are all on birth control…amazing!

Dan: You think there's a boom when the oil business draws 50,000 people a year to Dallas. You already get shortages of Sheetrock™. In the late seventies, there were drywall guys walking around wearing diamond earrings, hording building supplies in their rented warehouses.

In China's case, we're not talking about 50,000 people. In just a few years, we're talking about building from scratch a place the size of Dallas, Houston, San Antonio *and* New York City – and you can throw in Chicago, Atlanta and Miami.

You know how much iron, copper, nickel and cement that takes? Gee, you think it might produce a little black disgusting smoke? So whose neighborhoods are the mines and smelters and refineries going into? Yours? How about in France? Cape Cod?

I think I'll just wait until the regular people are scared out of the market by the temporary slowdown in the economy and then invest in the mines and refineries that are already there and buy in for a song. What do you think?

Franny: Well, I think you're having fun and making money.

What I like about the things that you're telling me, Dan, is that investing is really about being a world citizen. I mean, there's no way to avoid the way everyone is connected to everyone else. You just can't be an average American living on the checkerboard of *us* and *them* and still, as an investor, effectively give people what they want. You've *got* to become aware of the big picture. I really like that!

Dan: Glad to hear it. Are we done for today? I have to attend a piano recital.

Franny: We're done.

Points

- There are two approaches to investing. One is to find something you believe in as a way to use your capital to help people get what they want. Measure twice, cut once, and then stay with it through thick and thin.

- The other way is to speculate. Develop a strategy to lead the herd or to catch it moving in the wrong direction.

- Slowdowns in the economy, in production and in demand, when you see investors acting as a group and becoming increasingly frightened and panicked, are often the most profitable times to buy the stocks you want because the prices drop.

- Euphoric moments when everything about the economy seems perfect, and investors are acting as a group and are feeling very optimistic, are often excellent times to take your profits by selling stocks because the prices of the stocks include all the positive expectations, so the upside may be limited.

Massage Session #5

Franny: Oh, I'm running behind, but I see that Marcel took care of you. Are you all ready then?

Dan: I'm ready.

Franny: Great. How's that patella tendon? You haven't been straining it by wearing high heels, have you?

Dan: No.

Franny: Not everybody laughs at that joke. So, tell me, Dan The Moneyman, any exciting news since our last conversation about giving people what they want?

Dan: We were talking about Asia, weren't we?

Franny: Yes, and frankly, I didn't know all that stuff about China. Knowing it and thinking about it in terms of investing makes me feel a surge of possibilities, and it also makes me feel incredibly stymied. I mean, where to start? It's like having your sister-in-law with the plaid couches and daisy lampshades ask you to help her redecorate. There's so much to find out. What's underneath the rugs, the paneling and the coffee table that is a slice of pine tree with the bark still on it? What basic structure lies hidden from view? What's in her bank account? What do you really have to work with? And the biggest question of all: How far can you lead her down the silk road before she rebels and insists on earth tones and deer heads?

Dan: Are you asking for a way to start? A handle?

Franny: Yes! That's exactly what I'm saying.

Dan: One technique I have found, Ms. Gold, is to have an investment in something for which you have a real vision, and you stay with it through hell and high water like Travis at the Alamo. My guess is that you don't have a single stock in your portfolio that you know much about. On Wall Street, expert investors are watching what you and millions of other people do. Be like them: Stop watching the investments and start watching the investors.

When people start feeding off of one another's adrenaline, whether its fear, panic, greed or euphoria, they lose their minds. The problem with following the herd is that the herd is often wrong – especially at turning points where all the big money is made. When you listen to your friends, neighbors or even your financial advisor without scrutinizing the market for yourself, you lose money. That is something you can bet on.

It is human nature to settle in and believe that momentary conditions are going to go on forever, or for a long time. Once people are sold on the long-lasting movement type trend, they are too slow to spot the end of it. These movements often fall of their own weight. Once everybody is on board, we run out of new buyers. Take March 2000, for instance. At that point in time, everybody agreed on the new paradigm, but there was nobody left to buy it. The next seller found a shortage of buyers, and prices quickly collapsed.

On the other hand, how often have you seen skittish buyers abandon a good secular trend because they are afraid of what might come next? We all have the same human impulses. I have them, too; that's how I know how you feel.

In both cases, human nature is leading you astray. Your best fallback is to *study* the market, *evaluate* leading opinions and *act* as an individual. Like the billionaires – what we call the smart money – know that unless you see a compelling opportunity, your money *belongs in your pocket*. Remember, doing nothing is actually doing something.

Franny: So, study the market, evaluate opinions, and then act on my own judgment. Something tells me that this is more work than I'm used to.

Dan: Yes, it is. A problem that people have is *they want to make something for nothing*. They know there's no free lunch in their chosen profession, but for some reason, they expect easy money from mine. If you don't want to spend the time figuring out your own plan and executing it, then you'll just be at the mercy of financial middlemen, and your profits will be low.

You know how you wait until just the right moment to put pressure on my erectors spinae in my lower back? You gauge the pain and pliability of my muscles and you press down in just the right place at the right time?

Franny: I'm flattered! I didn't know that you noticed!

Dan: Of course I do. You are an expert at what you do. What you do is to use my body's conditions to your best advantage. Well, that's what I do with the herd. I use it to my best advantage. I make sure it's right where I want it, and then I either apply pressure (buy) or release pressure (sell).

To have our way with the crowd, we have to identify those times when normally intelligent individual investors are being swept away by crowd psychology. Since it's not practical to ask 200 million investors how they feel, I've worked very hard to come up with a way we can understand the crowd's psychological state.

The most accurate measurements I've developed over the years are based on some assumptions. Here's my thinking: The craziest investors in the world are options traders – investors who pay a premium to speculate in the options market. These options are highly leveraged, extremely volatile instruments that actually disappear into thin air if you hold them too long.

Franny: What's it like? Is it like a coupon?

Dan: It's a piece of paper where you pay for the right to buy or sell shares. Only time will tell if you actually do buy or sell them, but you pay a premium for that right anyway. Options can be used by pros to reduce risk in a whole slew of different ways, but it's pretty risky business for a speculator.

We've been able to gauge how scared, irrational or crazy investors are feeling by measuring the activities of options traders. We can infer their level of desperation from how much these highly emotional, often inexperienced speculators are willing to pay for a basket of options.

This measurement of investor panic or euphoria is called the **Index of Implied Volatility**. Although this is logical, experience has shown us that this data does not, by itself, give us clear signals. But we have found that we can process the data using a measurement called the **commodity channel.** The commodity channel compares the highest and lowest levels over a given period.

This is pretty complicated. I wouldn't expect someone like you to do it, but it gives you some idea of how the big guys do it.

The bottom line is we use it to gauge just how emotional and panicky investors feel when stocks are down or how euphoric and excited they feel when stock prices are running up.

Franny: Actually, it's very interesting. I think that I could gauge the options market if I understood it better.

Dan: Here's a very important point: We use this indicator differently, *depending on whether we believe we are in a bull or bear market*. During a bull market, moments of maximum fear and panic by the herd identify profitable entry points. However, when investors are happy, they're not crazy, they're correct.

During bear markets, the reverse is true. During bear markets, moments of overconfidence or complacency identify good selling or short-selling points, but you'd be promptly buried by trying to buy when the investors are showing fear. In a bear market, they're right to be scared, just as in a bull market, they're right to be happy and optimistic.

Franny: Bull, bear, bull, bear: one must memorize and strategize.

Dan: Firms that invest hundreds of millions of dollars have information that is way over the head of the average person. Playing against them is like fighting Mike Tyson. You know you can't get in the ring with a killer like Tyson and win. What you *can* do is create a plan, a strategy for how to use your capital to help people get what they want. Think it through when you're comfortable and relaxed, and then stick with it. The worst thing you can do after that is to make sudden changes to your long-term plan in the heat of battle.

Franny: It's like spotting someone with the "Dynasty Son Syndrome" and falling prey to his charms anyway. Your first plan was your best plan.

Dan: Did you say Dynasty Son Syndrome?

Franny: Never mind me. I was just sort of thinking out loud. Keep talking. I'm listening.

Dan: In many ways, we are still basically the same as our ancestors were a 100,000 years ago. Dangerous or tense situations still get our adrenaline flowing and still stimulate us to fight or run. That's why discipline is so difficult to achieve. In the heat of battle, when all your friends are investing in the newest cure for diabetes, you have powerful but unproductive urges to do the same thing. *The only way to win against the herd is to have a plan.* You should put it in writing, but you won't want to follow your plan! You won't want to buy when everybody's selling or sell something that everybody loves. But think about it. It stands to reason, if they habitually lose, the person who does the opposite must be winning. That's where you have to mentally check out of the herd and follow your plan. Otherwise, you'll lose money like everyone else.

Franny: This is really turning into quite a challenge. This will take up at least two hours a week of my time. I guess I can give up the soaps from India at three a.m. Perhaps, I can tune in on satellite to *Investment Opinions* from New Delhi instead. Anyho, I get that I have to bite the bullet rather than follow the crowd.

Dan: You call it "biting the bullet," I call it **discipline over conviction**. I do it. I follow my written plan to buy or sell at a certain point no matter what I believe at the moment. I hold onto that plan like a floatation device while the waves wash over me.

Once you figure out how to avoid being a part of the herd and how to use herd behavior to make money, then you still need to un-brainwash yourself. You've been conned by hired killers who call themselves "financial advisors."

Franny: You know, Dan, this actually jives really well with the way that I am. I'm cool with going against the herd, in theory, anyway. I am definitely in this groove.

Dan: Groovy, Ms. Gold. Actually, that folk singer you mentioned earlier, Tracy Chapman, isn't off base when she says that the devil is everywhere. One thing you've got to watch out for is what I call the "Financial Con Game."

When I say Financial Con Game, I'm referring to the fact that the financial world is *consciously* on a campaign to fool middle-class people. That doesn't mean that every single member of it is, but the whole thing is organized for that purpose. You see, there are really two financial businesses. One of them is what I think of as the *real* financial business. The real financial business consists of major companies, insurance companies and banks. It includes families with billions of dollars that have had money for generations. The real financial business encompasses a multitude of resources in the world, with a lot of it centered on Wall Street. The key here is that they are *investing their own money on behalf of themselves.*

When you think of people like Merrill Lynch, J.P. Morgan and CitiGroup, you may think of trading floors full of the smartest and brightest people. These people are sitting in loud rooms. You've probably seen something like this on television. They have clocks with the time zones all over the walls and multiple Bloomberg screens and all kinds of stuff on their tables. Each table has maybe five telephones. There are young people running back and forth and squawk boxes.

So based upon what you know of the financial world as it's been explained to you, given that you're supposed to buy a diversified portfolio and mutual funds and keep them, my question is, "What are all of those people doing in there?" Wouldn't they have been finished a long time ago?

Franny: Uh -huh.

Dan: Then, the next thing that you say to yourself is, "Why is my financial advisor (and I use that term loosely) not sitting in one of those rooms?" I'll tell you why. Your "financial advisor" is actually sitting on the freeway calling strangers all day. Am I right?

Franny: By god, you're right! Does this hurt?

Dan: Augh! Yes! What I'm saying is this guy is on the payroll. The bank or brokerage firm knows what his qualifications are. They know everything about him! They've got him as a resource, and they're willing to pay him. Tell me, how much do you think they consult with him on what they should do with their billions of dollars? They've got him on staff; they pay for his salary, right? Why don't they ask him what he thinks? Did you ever wonder? It seems like an obvious question, doesn't it?

Franny: Listening to you, I feel sort of daft. Why didn't I think of that? I thought I was good at questioning authority. I have a long history of throwing (marigold) peace seeds through military base fences. During the first Gulf War, I was arrested lying down in front of the State capitol in Austin. Not only that, but when I was living in Austin, I routinely submitted petitions for the impeachment of the City Council. You would think that I would question the whole obvious scam of the financial middleman guy, but it never even crossed my mind!

Dan: The truth is, Ms. Gold, that there's no chance that these big firms would do what they would want him to tell *you* to do. But you see there are actually *two* financial businesses. One of them is kind of glamorous and smart with highly educated, very rich guys who know how to really make money. These guys are involved in investment banking and global trading on behalf of the smart money. They move billions of dollars around. Of course, they want to be in the right place at the right time, and they try to get it right up to the second. That's what the institutions do with their money. Those guys are very interesting, right?

Franny: In a Dashiell Hammett sort of way.

Dan: Dashiell Hammett, the dashing playwright from the forties? Hmm…As I was saying, there's another financial world, which is what they want *you* to do with *your* money. In this scenario, the banks and brokerage houses pick retail people whom they don't believe know *anything;* otherwise, they would be asking them for their opinion. They want these retail people to go out there and tell you that there's *no way* that you can be in the right place at the right time. In fact, it's not even a worthwhile goal.

These large entities have even sponsored Nobel Prize-winning people for making up theories about how it's pointless for you to attempt to take appropriate action. They want you to believe that everything is a random walk.

Ask yourself this: If it's a random walk, why are they spending billions of dollars on the trading floor with all those people and all those squawk boxes? These big guys are not acting like it's a random walk; they're making *billions*.

The interesting thing is that every year you look at these guys whose net worth has gone up. I'm talking about CitiGroup, Merrill Lynch and all the big players. They're richer every year, and their worth has gone up. They made a ton of money in 2001 and 2002; they made a lot of profits, too. Why? Because they had bond trading. They moved their assets out of the stock market and made a lot of money on bonds. Then, they also made tons of money in 2003 because they were back in the stock market!

Franny: Whoa! This is like Watergate, man! Exposure! Gideon would love this. He would say, "Money's only paper, only ink/ We'll destroy ourselves if we can't agree/How the world turns/ Who made the sun/Who made the sea/The world we know will fall piece by piece."

Dan: Hmm…is that a song by…

Franny: Tracy Chapman. Yes. Dan, it's good to know what not to do, it really is. I'm getting real clear on the scam of the financial middleman.

Dan: Exactly. Aren't these the same guys who owned the tech stocks back in 2000? Well, how come they're still doing great? Obviously, the answer is that they are buying and selling stuff all the time, attempting to be in the right place at the right time. And they've got the very smartest people whose job it is to help them do that. *And yet, they're telling you to do exactly the opposite.*

The way they con you is to use a method called the *dyad*. A dyad is the putting together of two different ideas at one time, as if they were one idea. The idea is that your brain only has the horse-power to process one complicated question at a time. They open you up with item one, then slip in item two while the "door" is open.

Franny: Wait. Isn't a dyad part of creating an electrical charge? No. That's a diode. Never mind.

Dan: When you watch TV, you see the big players sponsor all sorts of financial programs. These programs involve the silent juxtaposition of the two types of people from the two different financial businesses. There are all these very glamorous and brilliant guys who understand the market and come in with independent ideas and use the very best in tools and millions of dollars in research. These glamorous guys come in and tell you what they find and what's going on and they're very cool, very witty.

The next guy who comes on is a retail salesman. You know in every city there are salespeople who are trying to pose as that kind of expert. In fact, they are salesmen who are actually working for the retail establishment owned by that same financial company. That same financial company that has that very sophisticated trading floor and trading operations and investment banking operations also has a retail establishment where they send salesmen to sell you stuff that *they would never in a million years put their money into*. What you see on these financial TV programs are salesmen who sell mutual funds and insurance. The large trading institutions are using these programs to make their retail salesmen appear to you as though they are the same as the glamorous, knowledgeable big players… and they aren't. They are slipping one in with the other, thinking that you won't know the difference. The sad part is that the average person usually doesn't know the difference, and they get conned.

Franny: Jeez Louise! I feel like I should be paying you instead of you paying me! We're almost done, but tell me this, what's in it for these guys?

Dan: What's in it for them is that they want to sell you all these products such as mutual funds and annuities. If you want to understand how it works, let's do this. Let's cut back to some of the concepts they use. For example, when they analyze a mutual fund they say, "This mutual fund has a lot of turnover, which is bad." Now, wait a minute. If I were to go to J.P. Morgan to borrow money for my company, they would want my financial statements. They would analyze me to see if I had a good business. They would think, in fact, that I was a high risk if I had low turnover. They would label my business as inefficient. I'm not using all of my resources with a low turnover because turnover means how many times I'm using the same thing in a year, right? Well, it seems that the world of selling mutual funds to regular people is the only place on the planet, the only industry, the only business where turnover is bad. In fact, the same company – if they were going to lend me money and were evaluating my business – would think that if I don't have turnover I'm no good. Yet here they are, trying to sell you on the idea that turnover is bad in the use of your assets.

Turnover means efficiency. Turnover means how efficiently are you using your assets?

So now let's talk about your business, which might be plumbing supplies or maybe the coin and stamp business.

Franny: Import/Export.

Dan: Import/Export. Of course, in your case, business turnover is good because what you want to do is get it in there and sell your merchandise: buy it wholesale and sell it retail. You don't necessarily want the highest price when you're selling. You don't want to buy it for the cheapest price. You just want to move goods. Turnover!

If I'm in the import/export business, I want turnover. My backer wants turnover. My wife wants me to have turnover. Everybody wants me to have turnover. Who is the one person who doesn't want me to have turnover? The *warehouseman* because he doesn't want me to have just the right stuff and sell it just in the nick of time. He wants me to have one of everything and keep it forever and **pay him rent**.

He doesn't care about me. He's not trying to get me to efficiently use my resources. *He's trying to get me to buy way too much inventory and then pay him to store it.* Is this starting to make sense to you? Isn't that what the mutual fund company is to you — a warehouse company where they take your money and put it into a little bit of everything, so that you don't move it. You keep paying them rent for holding it. Of course, they call turnover bad. But with their money, they don't want to do that. With their money, they want to get it in exactly the right place and move it by the second. *For them, turnover is good.* For you, they want to be the warehouseman — they're selling you storage!

So what they do is this: They send a guy out there who tells you, "You can't possibly know what you want. You can't possibly take appropriate action. There *is* no appropriate action. What you should do for safety's sake is to buy one of everything and keep it in my warehouse. Don't attempt to make appropriate rules, don't attempt to have inventory that is consistent with what is going on in the world. Just have one of everything and pay me to store it because you're too stupid to own the appropriate assets at the right time and sell them when they're no longer likely to make you money."

Franny: Not that I'm actually *stupid*, right? I'm just like *asleep*.

Dan: No, you're not stupid; you're just lulled into believing a lie.

Franny: Let's just say I do some homework and all, but I still need advice from someone who has more experience and education in these things than I have. How do I find an advisor who isn't just blowing smoke up my, uh…my whatever?

Dan: Good question! Let's save that for next time.

Franny: Great!

Points

- In bear markets, wait for moments of overconfidence or complacency. These times indicate good selling or short-selling points.

- During a bull market, wait for moments of maximum fear and panic by the herd. These times indicate profitable buying opportunities.

- Because you are the steward of your resources and also a member of the herd, it is very difficult to make judgments about the extreme feelings. Don't trust your feelings and beliefs. Choose to live your investing life based on discipline rather than convictions or beliefs.

- Create a strategic plan and write it down. Then stick to it. Exercise discipline over conviction. Follow your written plan to buy or sell at a certain point or when a certain event comes to pass, no matter what you believe or feel at that moment.

- There are actually *two* financial businesses. One of them is made up of sophisticated experienced, connected, informed pros who know how to really make money. These guys are involved in investment banking and global trading on behalf of the smart money. They move billions of dollars around.

- **The second financial business consists of salesmen who sell mutual funds, stocks at retail and insurance. The large trading institutions want to make their retail salesmen appear to you as though they are the same as the glamorous, knowledgeable big players... and they aren't. They are there to sell you on warehousing your money. Remember: they and their companies can do very well, whether you are making money or not!**

- **Turnover in any business is a measure of how efficiently assets are being used. Investing is no different from any other business. Instead of mindlessly avoiding turnover, make your judgment based on how it is being used. Excess activity designed to generate commissions for somebody else is, of course, inefficient and to be avoided. Activity that generates profit by bringing you into rhythm with the markets and the economy is the only way to generate profits for you. Seizing opportunities generates transactions. Undoing mistakes generates transactions. Taking advantage of inevitable changes in the economy or the business environment generates transactions.**

Massage Session #6

Franny: Hey, Dan The Moneyman, are you comfortable?

Dan: Yes.

Franny: Great. Hey, there's something I wanted to ask you from our discussion last time.

Dan: Sure.

Franny: If all these guys are warehousemen, how do I find the right kind of guy?

Dan: A lot of people ask me where they are going to find the right kind of guy.

People are desperately looking for the right mechanic to fix their Volkswagen; they're desperately looking for the right guy.

The reason people want to find someone to trust is so they can check their brains at the door. Finding a leader would make the life of a herd member much easier, wouldn't it?

The reason people want a leader is because that's a decision you only have to make once, and then life is easy, right? If you actually have to evaluate ideas, your job never ends. But the fact is that safety comes from doing the right thing rather than following the right leader.

You can use researchers, traders, managers, brokers. All these services help, but you have to make sure whatever they do is consistent with your ideas, that you firmly believe the actions they're taking are the highest and best use of your hard-earned capital. Get their ideas, think about them, and hire people to do what you would do if you had the time and information.

Secondly, it would help if you firmly believed that the right guy was someone who knew how to make money, not just store things. Isn't it true that when you started that relationship, and you were talking about financial planning or investment advice, that in the back of your mind there was some kind of idea that you were going to end up with *more money* **after** your investment than **before** your investment?

Isn't it true that now twenty years later, you seem to have suspended that requirement and you seem to be just looking for a warehouseman? What I'm telling you is that either you have to be in the right place at the right time or find somebody who shares your vision to be in the right place at the right time *or* put your money in your pocket. Whatever you do, do not store it in a place where people have no idea what they're doing. For the past six years, people who just invested in a diversified portfolio have been seeing their values fluctuate sporadically and end up just moving sideways. In fact, people with diversified portfolios of stocks or mutual funds haven't made any money in eight years now.

Rich people believe that the default place for their money is in their pocket. They don't believe that because they only have so many years to retirement their money has to be deployed all the time whether it's a good deal or not. That's what *you* believe, thanks to the retail salesman guy.

Basically, it is this belief that he has about storing money in mutual funds that makes his company not care what he thinks, right? His company wants its money to be in exactly the right place at the right time, or they want it deployed where it will make some kind of interim earnings while they wait for the right place at the right time. They just observe this funny rule, where they insist on being paid for the use of their money. What nerve, right?

They do nothing when they don't have a great idea because they know that *sooner or later another opportunity will arise and they want to have the cash*. They don't believe in activity for the sake of activity. That's why billionaires seldom get poorer.

Franny: What am I supposed to do about it?

Dan: I would say the first thing that you should do, if you don't know what to do, is to *declare a moratorium on all financial actions*. Go to cash! Get rid of all that crap. Adopt the policy that the only time that you're going to commit resources is when you personally have a real significant and important conviction that by deploying your resources – by investing your money – you're going to come out with more money than you started with, and *significantly* more money. You must hold a strong conviction that you're going to be paid for the risk, you must understand how, and you must have a specific exit strategy.

Franny: What if I told you that I don't have time to do all of that?

Dan: You know, I knew you'd say that. I wanted to talk about this because your whole life will change when you GET this.

Let's look at this a few different ways. First of all, saying that you don't have the time is a rationalization, and you're just repeating it because that's what the group says. The truth is that if I came to you at your house and wanted you to invest 3,000 dollars in a new convenience store that I want to open (not your entire life savings, just 3,000 dollars), you'd investigate carefully before you would be willing to participate in that. You'd never just put money in without knowing everything about the project, because you're at your house and you know how to behave, and you're not intimidated in that situation. You're not

90

going to put a cent in the project until you *really* understand the deal.

You would find out *everything* about me and my convenience store. You would talk to my banker. You'd sit and look at the location for *hours* to determine if it's a good place. You would know all about my plans; you would know about everything before you commit three grand to it! If I told you "Hurry up!" because you were approaching retirement, you'd say, "I'm not doing this without thinking about it. We might as well get that straight right now." You know how to behave appropriately in that social situation, don't you?

The investment in paper scenario is just exactly the same, but it's a social situation in which you are less confident. It's not that you don't know how to behave; it's that you have *forgotten*. Again, you're being a member of the herd and you're moving along the chute to the slaughter not realizing that this is America and you don't have to do any of that.

Franny: OK. Shift a little on your left side. You really shot holes in my resistance. I have to tell you that the desire to get something for nothing is huge. It feels like a steamroller inside of me. I have so much inertia around doing the work necessary to make money with investments. Is it terribly hard to find a good company or group of them?

Dan: The fact is that there are plenty of things for you to invest in that make perfect sense. You don't have to be an expert on everything. But I guarantee that if you wanted to find out about a certain company, a certain bond or a certain thing, and you were willing to take a little time and go to the library or ask questions of people who are positioned to actually know, within thirty days you could be one of the world's foremost experts on that one subject. I absolutely know that. You may not know about everything else, but you could read through and know about that one thing, and know as much about it as anybody else on the planet. You would know at *least* enough to decide whether it was appropriate and know that course of action was what you wanted to do.

And you really only need a few investments. You don't have to be an expert on everything.

And so, if somebody's been doing things for you indefinitely and you trust them, that's great. Otherwise, it is incumbent on you to understand every single thing you invest in totally. If you don't understand it totally, don't do it. *Don't do it.*

Franny: What should I do instead?

Dan: I don't know what you should do, but I can tell you what I do. I stand back, keep myself awake, and every once in while an idea comes to me. I just see something that people are going to want and need.

Like in September 2005, I was getting ready for the economy to slow down. I was gradually selling off all my copper and iron mining companies every time people would act exuberant and run up the prices of those stocks. I had figured that with the Fed raising interest rates, the price of oil getting high enough for people to start being upset by it, and just the age of the bull market, it was getting risky to own stocks that depend on world growth. Chinese demand kept the prices of construction-related raw materials high, but what if China slowed down a little?

When that horrible hurricane hit the Gulf Coast, I couldn't really predict how it would affect our lives, but it seemed logical that at first we'd get a slowdown as everything just ground to a halt. But the one thing I knew was soon there would be a huge amount of new construction to rebuild. I didn't know what they'd rebuild or how they'd do it. I didn't want to invest in home builders because they have exposure all over the country, not just in the storm area. I didn't want to invest in general diversified industrials, like some growth mutual fund, because I couldn't yet see how the whole economy would be affected. But I knew whatever they did, they'd need lots and lots of copper for electric wires, and they'd need iron and steel.

So even though I wasn't ready to invest in stocks in general, and even though the herd was probably due to get more scared and drive stock prices down further, I decided to buy a couple of companies that operated copper and iron mines.

I looked at pictures of the price charts of some mining companies, and I found the ones that seemed to go up and down in lockstep with people's expectations about the economy. Then I researched those companies – to see what they were saying about themselves. I also read up on what the top analysts were saying about them, to see if I could find anything bad about the way they were running their business. I subscribe to a lot of expensive information to save a little time, Ms. Gold, but the truth is, all this company information is available for free on the Internet, if you want to take the time to find it.

Franny: Yes, I was looking at some articles just the other day.

Dan: After all that research, I finally settled on an iron mine from South America because steel is made from iron, and I found the copper mining company whose stock had moved the most in the early stages of the last bull market.

Now I had to make a plan about how I'd buy and sell them. Since those stocks had just been coming down in price, I thought maybe they were ready to buy right then. I couldn't tell, though, whether people would panic further as the story unfolded. So I put about three percent of my stock money into each of those two companies. If the stocks started to rise, I'd be happy enough with that. I'm not greedy. But if people continued to feel more distressed and drove the prices down further, I had room to deploy another two or three percent later at the peak of panic.

Franny: Good. Cool head.

Dan: I considered it inevitable that demand for copper and iron would develop, so I decided that no amount of fear would cause me to sell those stocks at a loss. I decided that the only way I'd sell those stocks for a loss would be if I found out something horrible about those particular companies or their management.

Franny: You must realize, Mr. Moneyman, not all of us can dance like Fred Astaire. I mean, I'm lucky if I have the energy to reread Thomas Wolfe twice a year.

Dan: Thomas Wolfe?

Franny: *Look Homeward Angel.* It's a great book; American literature at its best.

Dan: OK. You say you don't have the time, that you're not as good at doing the research as I am, but I'll bet you, Ms. Gold, that you spend more time perfecting your plan for how to get a good deal on a five-hundred dollar weekend trip to Cancun than I did researching the iron mine in South America. You look at pictures of the hotels, you get details about every little amenity, what meals are included… and I know you put more effort into picking your widescreen, high-definition TV – comparing the contrast ratio, how many pixels and all that for the money. You put more effort into those things than you've ever spent planning the investments you risk your life savings on. You see, it's all a matter of confidence and priorities, not about time.

Franny: Hmm. You have a point there. I did spend like four hours studying feng shui and then another four hours rearranging the furniture in my house and putting mirrors and fountains in the right places.

Dan: OK. Feng shui, not high-definition TV, but you get my point.

Franny: Yep, I get your point… Alright, you're good to go, Dan The Moneyman. Keep doing your bends and stretches, and I'll see you next week.

Points

- People look for a financial advisor, often, so they can check their brains at the door. Don't rely on someone else to lead you. Decide what your priorities are, establish your plan, learn how to evaluate and then if you want to hire someone to do the work, you can.

- In sideways markets, such as the one the United States has experienced over the past eight years, diversification simply means being pretty wrong all the time. People who have held on to diversified portfolios of stocks or mutual funds haven't made any money in eight years because the value of stocks in general has not risen during that period.

- Successful investors do nothing when they don't have a great idea because they know that *sooner or later another opportunity will arise and they want to have the cash*. They don't believe in activity for the sake of activity.

- Adopt the policy that the only time you're going to commit resources is when you personally have a significant and important conviction that by making that move you're going to come out with more money than you started with and *significantly* more money. You must hold a strong conviction that you're going to be paid for the risk and you must understand how.

- Make sure you have an exit strategy that is just as specific as your entrance strategy. Most people can trace their lack of investing success to problems with selling, not to problems with buying.

- You have time for anything you feel good about, including movies, TV sports, shopping and research on vacations. Saying you don't have time to research your investments is a rationalization, and you're just repeating it because that's what the group says. It's all a matter of confidence and priorities, not about time.

- You could know more than most people about a company or an industry in thirty days if you simply went to the library and onto the Internet.

- If you don't feel totally sure and informed about an investment decision, don't do it.

Franny and Gideon

Franny: I'm at my house making a kind of Kim Chee using my crock pot when Gideon stops by. He wants the latest update on Dan The Moneyman's ongoing advice. Every time I tell Gideon what Dan says, I get the feeling that he's not too surprised. It's as if he knows what Dan's going to say before he says it. It's like he's already read the guy's autobiography or something. I attribute this to the fact that he's just very weird. "Why worry?" is my other life philosophy.

I tell him the whole deal, how we're being scammed by the middlemen, how we've been lulled by the Fed dyads and how we need to have the courage of our convictions to figure out what we want to invest in by staying awake, avoiding being swept away by the call of the herd and thinking clearly about how to use our capital to help people get what they want. Then, planning ahead about when it will be time to buy or sell.

"So, what's your plan?" he says to me. I pause.

"I really don't know."

"What are you passionate about?"

"Developing countries."

"What about developing countries?"

"The people, their freedom from poverty."

"What does that boil down to for you?" I gave him a long, hard look. Who was this man in my kitchen prying into my soul? I found it a little thrilling.

"What does it boil down to? Well, for me, it boils down to birth control."

"Great. What sort of birth control? All of them?"

"No. No. I'm not too keen on the pill these days. Actually, the copper wire IUD is proven to be the safest and the most effective form of birth control. It got a bad rap for a few months in the 80s, but it's really effective and safe."

"OK. What do you know about IUDs? What do you know about copper wire? What do you know about effective distribution agencies in developing countries?"

I cut into a box of rock salt methodically. "Nothing. Absolutely nothing."

"Do you think there's a chance you might be able to make some money investing in one or all of these industries?" I nodded, my eyes on the floor. Gideon, miracle Dynasty Son, Gideon was being sort of masterful and sweet. I stared at his toes in his sandals. Actually, he wasn't too bad-looking for a white guy.

He put his hand up to his lips like a cigar and did a Groucho Marx impression. "Do you want I should help you?"

This was a spin; a spin on my shift. "Umm…OK. Are you talking about research?" He nodded.

"You want to take copper wire and I'll take IUD distribution?" He nodded with his green eyes on me.

"I just noticed that we have the same color eyes," he says, looking deep into mine. Something told me to let it go for now. If the time ever came for me to confess that I am a blue-eyed blonde to this refugee from Malibu, now was not it.

To make a long story short, Gideon and I set up a research model, and I actually went to bed dreaming of kayaks, Spanish cathedrals and family planning.

Massage Session #7

Franny: Dan! You're back!

Dan: You seem excited to see me, Ms. Gold.

Franny: Yes, get ready. I'll be back in a few.

(Six or seven minutes later)

I've got news for you! I've started researching industries I'm interested in. Gideon and I have a plan. What do you think of that?

Dan: Not bad. You're a fast learner.

Franny: Time is money.

Dan: Well, yes and no. Mmm…yes, right there; it is very tight.

The first thing that you should do is say, "My money belongs in my pocket. I do not have to do anything unless it is a totally good idea. The truth is that I don't have to put my money into a diversified portfolio or mutual fund, and in fact, the chances are that a diversified portfolio or mutual funds will be worth less a year from now than today."

That being the case, because we're in that kind of a market, *it would absolutely be better for you to do nothing than put your money into a diversified portfolio of mutual funds* if you're not capable of knowing when it's good to invest and when it's bad.

There are all kinds of people who are very good at knowing when to invest and when not to invest. You *can* get good at it. This is about how you can get good at it yourself. You can think things through; you can get good at this. You can develop the mental process to be able to do it. If you can't invest it in absentee securities, every bit of your money needs to be with enterprises that you know. Not one penny of it should be in stocks that you don't know anything about! Not one cent!

It's not radical to think this way if you're a billionaire. You may only think this is radical because you're indoctrinated with that silly retail con-man stuff. Let me point something out to you about all these insurance agents, all these mutual fund salesmen, all this stuff that's on Yahoo, all the P/E ratios, all the CNN, NBC information and all the stuff that you're saying that I'm contradicting.

Let's do a little exercise. You know I'm a scientific kind of guy, a mathematical kind of guy. So if I want to know if there's a corre-lation between two things, the first thing I do is make a picture of the two things and I look at the pictures to see if they're similar.

If they're similar, one's causing the other one maybe, or they're both being caused by the same thing, but they may have some correlation. If the pictures do not relate to each other in any way, I would say, "You know, it looks to me like these two factors don't have anything to do with each other." Right?

Franny: I'm following you so far.

Dan: OK. This is a good way to test theory. Let's think about CNN or NBC news magazine, the last book you read, the salesman who comes up to your house to talk about mutual funds, the P/E ratios that you get and all that stuff. Do you know how many hundreds of millions of people now have access to that information? They get it on the Internet, on Yahoo and on CNN or NBC. They listen to it, and they get it all over the place. Salesmen come out to teach it to them, right? There are magazines about it. If I wanted to test the value of that information I would say, "Well, the only possible value of this information *must* be that it helps people get richer, right?"

All this free information is now ubiquitous. Hundreds and millions of people get this information for free every day. So, as a mathematician, I have to ask you, *where are all the rich people?*

Franny: Except for the guys at this club, I don't know any.

(Dan starts tracing in the air with his finger under the massage table.)

Dan: I'm going to draw a picture for you of the number of people who have received free information on the P/E ratio, the profits and all that stuff, and been reached by insurance salesmen and mutual fund salesmen. Then I will draw you this exponential curve in the shape of a *J* of those people who have been exposed to this onslaught of data.

Now, I ask you, if this was all very valuable, wouldn't you expect that the wealth of that population would also show up as a *J*?... Does it?... What does this tell you?... To check my methods, let's think about this: How about if I wanted to draw a picture of the wealth of the people who disseminate this information to the middle-class? What about them? Is their wealth increasing in the shape of a *J*?

The mutual fund companies, CitiGroup, Merrill Lynch, etc.: Does their wealth follow the curve of the dissemination? What we learned from this very simple scientific exercise, that any person could have done at home, was that the *benefit* of all this informa-tion is to the people who are **sending it out**, *not* to the people who are receiving it.

When I tell you something and you say, "How revolutionary that is. It flies in the face of all the bogus information that I've been hearing in the media." Well, all I can tell you is that there is a curve that is very meaningful between the people who believe what I believe and wealth.

Franny: Hmm. I really should sell out of all those mutual funds I bought without knowing what's in them. I'm earning some money, but then the next year, I lose it. What you say is that the best place for my money is in my pocket, unless I really see a compelling opportunity.

It is rather radical, although if I were a billionaire…if I *were* a billionaire, I'd have a free-of-charge elementary school in Mali and one in Mississippi, too. Why not? It's a state of unrealized potential if you don't count the blues. Anyho, if I were a billionaire, my money and mind would be one, not farmed out. It's neurotic the way I'm so disconnected from my money; it really is.

Dan: Yes, it is neurotic, Ms. Gold. Kind of dependent, but you can change that. If you'd just stop losing money; if you take all the money that you've lost over the years by being negligent and dependent, and you compounded that interest, you'd be a hell of a lot better off than you are right now. That's Number One. Even if you just stopped losing money on things you didn't really believe in anyway, you'd be better off. That may not be a satisfying answer to you, but it is a 100 percent true one. Stop being conned!

Franny: I want to stop, but I'm still not confident of what I should do instead. I think I'm on the right track…

Dan: The question "I want to stop but what should I do instead?" is the question of a victim. It is the question of a battered woman who is being asked, "How many more chances are you going to give him?" At some point, you have to go for yourself. You have to say, "For my own sanity I'm going to get rid of this husband."

You say, "Yes, but my children need a father. Yes, but he promises that he won't do it again, and he's so sorry. I can see he's so sorry."

You're saying to yourself that you've got to give him another chance. At some point, the authorities and people who care will say to you, "You must be insane!" Right? Maybe he will get better, more power to him. We hope he does, but for your sanity, you've got to move on.

Do you understand? You've got to draw the line somewhere and say, "That was the last beating, period!"

The battered woman says, "Yes, but I'm going to be alone. Who am I going to go to the movies with?"

I don't know who you're going to go to the movies with, but to stop getting beaten is the first step. Let's stop getting beaten! Not only that, but I can truthfully tell you that you will never find someone to go to the movies with who doesn't beat you until you get rid of him.

Franny: Oh, that is so, so true. You don't know how many women actually say that! It's amazing.

Dan: You don't say that?

Franny: Me? Oh, not really. I've got my two life philosophies, "Get over it," and "Why worry?" They get me through most relationships. Whenever I get a Tarot reading, I'm always Isis: strong, calm, queenly in a way. That's me.

Dan: I see. But, in terms of investing your money you're saying, "I don't know where to go!"

I'm saying that I don't know how to fix that right now. All I'm telling you is that you're standing in the middle of the freeway. If you don't get out of the freeway, you're going to be dead. Get out of the freeway, and then we'll figure out where to go.

You're tying the two ideas, *moving* and *where to move*, together because you're such a victim, such a confirmed victim. You think because you don't know the alternative that you have to stay there and get killed. You see how pathetic that is? I'm not trying to insult you. I just want you to stop being conned. You need to tie the beaten wife together with being conned. There's no connection there.

You linked two concepts together without differentiating between them, *leaving* and *choosing another place to invest your money*. That's because they've been linked in your mind by those people who link together stories. That's how insurance and financial products are sold to you.

The large companies that sell financial advice are the best propagandists since the Simbionese Liberation Army. Do you know who that is?

Franny: Yeah. Patty Hearst.

Dan: Right. Anyway, they were the group who kidnapped Patty Hearst. I would call you a victim of the Patty Hearst Syndrome. You know how they did it? They made her stand in a closet and repeat these outrageous communist ideas. After awhile, she was in there robbing banks with them. You see, you buy into it when they take you, isolate you, break down your reality and have you repeat the misinformation long enough.

The big guys appreciate what I'm saying. For instance, ninety percent of the people at CitiGroup are not involved in its retail brokerage. They happen to have Smith Barney, which is kind of like a gang of marauders, but most of CitiGroup is involved in normal banking activity. In fact, CitiGroup just sold their Travelers unit. Hibernia Bank is selling their Prudential unit. American Express is selling off their financial planning unit. Do you know why? Because they used to rely on this gimmick where they would present the side of their business that was there to lend you money and do the consumer services, and they would use that to get into your house and heart and then try to sell you their crap that they sell, the insurance and annuities under the guise of financial planning or estate planning. Now, it isn't working very well for them anymore.

It used to be that they would get you in there with the credit card, and then their guys would come and sell you annuities, life insurance, mutual funds with loads – anything they could think of. People are so sophisticated now about conflict of interest that the bait and switch just doesn't work anymore. So what are those big financial giants doing? They are sticking with the real business and leaving the financial planning to somebody else. I'm telling you, it's not only me who knows this stuff. *It's everybody but you*. Everyone with a lot of money knows all of it. It's true.

I know exactly what they're doing because much earlier in life, I was one of them – a hired gun for a big financial institution.

You know, there really isn't anywhere else to start out and gain experience but on Wall Street. Just about everybody comes up through that mill. In fact, I don't really see myself as any more moral than the retail hired guns out there.

With a whole retail industry that evolved based on a big lie, I just got lucky and found out telling people the truth actually is a more lucrative business model. When you think about it, it's kinda funny that we've gone so far in that direction, with all the financial media, and all the baloney. Telling people the truth has actually created a unique niche.

I have an open forum on my radio show. When a question or a discussion of this stuff comes up, I literally beg someone who does this stuff to call in and argue or refute what I'm telling you now. Do you know how many times that has happened in all these years of prime time radio? Zero, never, not once. They're all listening; they all know what I say. They come to hear me speak, and they even come up and say "Hello." They follow my investment strategies, but they know very well that what I'm telling you is absolutely true, and so no one ever calls to contradict me on this.

Franny: Yeah, I listen to your show sometimes. It's funny how once the business is over and they've scammed as much money as they can from the little guy, they don't mind if you talk about it on the radio. That's big of them.

Dan: You could look at it that way. You have a point. I guess the people who suspect, or know the truth, and live the lie every day, still find it entertaining. Remember: These guys aren't really experts on finance.

They're trained salesmen, and most of them only know what they learn from their company's training program. In fact, Ms. Gold, a lot of those sales people on the retail side started out to really help make people's lives better. They answered an ad for a sales job that promised them a career, and they've been trained to sell what their big investment bank or financial institution wants them to sell. You know, if they set out to be thieves, they could have just burgled houses. They didn't have to be members of the United Way and work as hard as they do. I know what they're going through, but remember: I grew up on the real finance side of Wall Street, so when I was in their position, I could see what was going on.

Franny: So, speaking of the *real* Wall Street, let me tell you what I'm doing. I'm passionate about birth control in developing countries, mainly copper wire IUDs. I'm researching IUD distribution in these countries, and Gideon is researching the copper wire used to manufacture IUDs. What do you think of that?

Dan: Good for you! Helping people get what they want is another good test of investments. Because the fact is that if you can take your capital and deploy it in such a way that you help a lot of people get what they want, there's a very good chance that you're going to be well rewarded for doing that.

Particularly if you're one of the first people to see it, or you're one of the people who are willing to finance something when few others are willing to take the risk. For example, I'm making some investments right now, as stock prices plummet, in a couple of companies that sell low-grade uranium to nuclear power plants, an idea I got from the investment guru Tobin Smith. I am putting some money into that because it's only a matter of time. What I'm doing is helping to capitalize on something and helping people get what they want. People are feeling unwilling to look ahead right now. They're acting as though the whole world economy will grind to a halt, led by a crashing U.S. economy.

If I weren't thinking, I'd be scared along with them. The news is full of facts that support the theory that things are slowing down. But standing back a little, I know that nothing is going to stop the Americans from rebuilding the Gulf Coast. Nothing will stop the Chinese from developing their cities and moving hundreds of millions of their people up to the middle class. The same is true in India, Latin America and even Africa. Much of this development is being led by governments that don't even care about getting a good deal. They follow their plans regardless of economic conditions. A horrible economy might put all this development off for a year or so, somewhere along the line, but it's all going to happen no matter what!

There's no doubt in my mind that whatever the zoning problems are in the United States the world will be generating a lot of electricity with nuclear power. It just isn't practical to generate all that electricity with oil and gas, and coal is dirty. So there will be lots of nuclear power generating electricity, and everyone will need more and more uranium. The price of uranium has doubled in the last year or so, and this is just the beginning. I can't think of a safer way to make a fortune than to buy uranium producers when their stocks are being sold wholesale by a herd of panicked amateur investors.

If you apply that to how people made so much money in technology, think about what was going on in March 2000. Everybody was lining up to put money into a few stocks that already had enough money, right? Those technology companies weren't selling stock to the public. Their public offerings were already done, but people were still speculating – buying the stock from each other. In fact, there was so much demand for stocks in those areas that the investment banking community was rounding up with every bunch of kids in a dorm in Austin or Oakland or San Jose who could write software and taking them public. All they really cared about was keeping up with the demand for tech stocks.

They did this because there weren't enough technology stocks to go around, and everybody wanted them. They created over-capacity – too much stock in too many companies – and many of these companies really had no economic reason to exist.

The investment bankers got rich helping those speculators and investors get what they wanted – tech stocks. But those speculators forgot about helping the world get what it wants and needs. They were simply jumping on a train. They were worried about *themselves,* not the world. It was that childish greed – trying to follow along and basically get something for nothing. They didn't think they were helping anybody get what they want. They thought they had a chance to make some easy money for nothing. So, they were jumping on that. In a time when stocks are out of style and the stock market is not doing to well, I'll take my capital and invest it in a company that supplies low-grade uranium. The company then sells this low-grade uranium to power plants so people will be able to find alternative ways to power their houses, factories, offices and schools. This is an investment where I'm asking myself, "What does the world want and need?"

All I'm saying is that the economy works this way. Our society rewards you for helping people get what they want. People got on a bandwagon to put money into companies that already had more than enough money, right? It was a bunch of greedy people buying and selling to each other, and in the end, they got what society generally pays people for naively jumping on a full train. It wasn't very pretty. *What our society pays people to do is to help other people get what they want.*

By the way, one of the worst-paying jobs in our society is going around telling people what they *need*, right? Ask your insurance agent or your ex-husband about how much we reward people for telling them what they need. Personally, I like to stick to what people want and avoid betting on what I think they need.

My observation, Ms. Gold, is that people actually do get what they want most of the time. That's why people who can't even pay for their kids' schooling and barely have enough money for the rent have the very best cell phone that takes pictures. It's unbelievable! They need tuition money; textbooks and toys and the telephone is what they want. First, everybody gets what they want. So I focus on what people want and forget about what I think they need. If I do that with courage and intelligence, I'm going to be rewarded, and I promise if you do nothing but use your capital to help people get what they want and you do it carefully, you'll be a very rich young lady. That's THE test for a long-term investment.

Franny: That's like my friend, Eva, who bought a hair salon near the Four Seasons Retirement Center in L.A. It wasn't long before she figured out that these ladies didn't want their hair done, they just wanted hair. It's Eva's Wig Salon, and she does a booming business.

Dan: Eva gave them what they wanted. By the way, Ms. Gold, this is the secret you've been searching for since the day we met! In fact, this is one of the main reasons that I got almost completely out of the stock market in the last few years. I've had about thirty percent of the money under my control in the stock market since 2001.

Seventy percent of that money has been in complicated bonds, which are making somewhere in the nine to eleven percent range. They're somewhat complicated. In my view, they're not very risky at all. I did that because I felt the world didn't need a lot of money put into companies over the past few years.

I'm developing a new bond strategy for 2006 and into 2007.

Franny: Great. Is this something I can actually do right now?

Dan: I think you can follow this thinking. Let's try. It starts with the idea that Americans borrow a lot of money from abroad, that the American baby-boom generation is aging and getting tired of real hard work, and that the younger replacement generation is much smaller. In the past, this has been a recipe for a slowing economy. Look at Japan during the nineties.

It stands to reason that the dollar would be getting weaker against the currencies of the dynamically growing Asian countries and probably other emerging economies as well. That's exactly what has been happening until 2005. But the U.S. Federal Reserve has been steadily raising interest rates, and that has attracted capital from foreign investors and served to strengthen the dollar, temporarily.

In early 2006, it looks very much like the Fed will soon stop raising interest rates and the dollar will probably start to fall in value again, compared to those dynamic, fast-growing currencies like China, South Korea, maybe even Brazil and Venezuela. Interest rates will be going lower here. We spend more dollars in their countries than they spend in ours. You can think of a handful of other reasons why this is almost inevitable.

So, Ms. Gold, why not buy bonds from safe, democratic countries that do lots of business with China and India? High-quality, safe bonds, denominated in those foreign currencies. I'm looking at New Zealand, Australia, South Korea and maybe even Japan.

As China and India grow, these countries will be making a fortune dealing with them, just as many Americans will. But our dollar will be going down, which means, to us, the foreign currencies will be going up. Instead of just trading currency, we get a guarantee of getting our principal back. I think there's little question that at some point soon, those foreign countries' money will have gone up against ours.

The best part is because we get a fair rate of interest, we don't have to be in a rush. We can afford to wait patiently for our moment. We'll get back our original principal, our interest as planned and all the gains from the change in currency values.

Franny: That sounds fabulous, and you know, I actually understand it! But what I still don't get, though, Dan, is why I have to get so smart. Why can't I just throw my money into some funds and let it grow? Why isn't the stock market so good anymore? My grandfather and mom swore by it.

Dan: Good question. It'll be good again, don't worry. The market goes through these fifteen- and twenty-past-year cycles all the time. In the last ten years, the make-up of the stock market has changed dramatically. I look at the companies out there now, and I see many companies with expertise in many things. It used to be — in the late nineties — if you knew how to write software or you had a device that made people more productive, you had a monopoly. People had to come to you. They had to pay any amount of money because you made them more productive and helped them compete. Profit margins were enormous. Sales were going up 100 percent a year. It was fabulous! That's why those companies attracted all that capital, and their stock prices soared.

Now we live in a much tougher world. Nobody really has a monopoly anymore. People all over the world have figured out how to do just about everything a hundred different ways. So whatever a company does, there is somebody in Brussels, somebody in China, South America or Africa that wants to do it cheaper. Everybody knows how to do the same stuff. *No matter what you do, there is somebody who wants to do what you do, and they want to do it cheaper.*

You want to raise your price one percent? If you do, your customers can go on the Internet and find out everything about your competitor in minutes. It's a helluva time to be a consumer.

Franny: Oh my gosh, yes. My girlfriend's husband keeps buying busts on the Internet. I think busts of important people used to be too expensive to buy and have shipped. Now he has a bust on every surface. He has a bust of all the presidents that he likes and one of Jimi Hendrix, Janis Joplin and all the great writers, of course. She hasn't said anything because she thinks he's working out something about his own grandeur. I don't know. The place is sort of creepy, but, yeah, it's all about the abundance of vendors. It's so cheap!

Dan: If it's so cheap, it's because there are so many vendors who sell it. Nobody's got a monopoly. You try to raise your price by one percent and they can go to somebody else, right? It's a wonderful time to be a consumer. Doesn't that make it a horrible time to be a vendor?

So, why in the world would I want to invest money in companies that have to kill themselves to survive in such a competitive world? See, you're trying to buy a diversified portfolio of mutual funds. You're worried about when you retire. I'm telling you that as long as the world's the way it is today, **you are not going to make any money** by pouring money into companies that are just fighting to survive. You see that? *You're not helping people get what they want.* We have enough companies in most fields. We just don't need more.

Now, of course, there will always be winners, and somebody is always in a bull market. You just have to be very targeted now. A scattergun approach just won't work in such a selective situation.

Franny: Diversified kinda means scattergun, doesn't it? I didn't look at it that way. I thought the right thing to do was diversify so I wouldn't make a mistake. Now you're telling me I have to be very precise. That isn't going to be easy to do.

Dan: I've been at it all my life, and it's hard for me, too – the game is very error-prone, but you generally can't win any game by playing not to lose. That's why I decided to be the banker. Instead of banging my head against the wall in cutthroat competition, just fighting to survive, I'd just be the lender. The companies kill themselves trying to squeak out a tiny profit; I get paid first. I don't have to worry who wins; I just have to figure out who will be able to pay me back. It's a much easier job. Just like your banker, he doesn't care if you're the best massage therapist; he just has to make sure you'll be able and willing to pay him back.

Here's what I know from being around this all my life. I mentioned cycles before — everything works in cycles. And you and I have all the time in the world. So after the competitors get thinned out because so many fail in this tough environment, and there are only a few companies left standing, and when companies are selling for the cash they have in the bank, and nobody wants to touch stocks with a ten-foot pole — after all that, I'll be interested in being a speculator again. I've been through this more than once, Ms. Gold, and though the events are different each time, the feel is remarkably similar.

Franny: Every time I hear what you're saying, I really like it. At the same time, I feel like I missed the boat. I shouldn't kick myself, should I? I mean, I've spent my time perfecting other skills. I'm not a bad massage therapist, am I?

Dan: Not bad at all. In fact, Ms. Gold, you are the best massage therapist I've ever had. You have hands of gold.

Franny: Very funny. Get dressed and do your yoga. I'll see you next time, and I'll have more to report then.

Points

- Sometimes the most often repeated homilies are wrong. "You can't time the market!" is one of these. The fact is, human life is so short that almost nothing matters besides being in the right place at the right time or at very least, avoiding the wrong place at the wrong time.

- When you invest in bonds, you are the lender, not the vendor. You just determine who can pay you back rather than who will win the game. Because everyone is playing the game, everyone needs a lender.

- Allowing yourself to be limited to stocks and excluding bonds is like a football team that can only pass and has no running game. Such a team is always at a disadvantage. The world's bond market is ten times the size of the world's stock market and is the place where most of the world's smart money is held most of the time.

- The stock market has changed dramatically from the days when you could simply invest and wait and make money. Today, no one has a monopoly over goods or services. Profit margins in many areas are very narrow, and stiff global competition has created a market where companies struggle to survive unless they are able to provide unique access to something the world wants and needs.

- There will always be opportunities for people with capital, but when the general long-term direction of the market is sideways, as it has been for the past eight years, you must tenaciously hold out for good deals before you invest.

- Any business starts with buying wholesale and selling retail. You can accomplish this in two ways. By:

    ◆ Recognizing important innovation and investing early,

    or

    ◆ Buying when the herd is in panic and selling when the herd is feeling happy and euphoric.

- Like the super rich, your money belongs in your pocket, to be deployed only when you have a compelling idea and a solid plan.

- Every bit of your money needs to be with enterprises that you know. Not one penny of it should be in things you don't know anything about! Not one cent!

- If all of the financial information that the TV networks, financial middlemen and other media put out were true, wouldn't most of the people who listened to it be rich? Wake up!

  The big investment firms will show you quickly that everything they do is designed to time the markets and that they profitably spend billions of dollars every year to get better and better at it.

- Think of yourself as the world's banker. You have capital to risk when the deal is irresistible, but as a staple, you lend money to earn interest. That means you train yourself to think bonds as well as stocks.

Franny and Gideon

Franny: OK. So I go home and I tell Gideon, "Jeez, I feel like the guy who missed the train in four different cities. Why didn't I know this stuff?"

He just shrugs and gives me a wink, "Get over it." You gotta love a guy who uses your own life philosophy on you. (I'm not actually in love with him.)

He reports that copper spring manufacturing is SIC code 3489. He goes on to tell me all about evaluating firms based on the factory machine replacement costs, and how much profit they make on a sale and the future demand for their products and the competition they face. I'm like, "What about your job? When did you have time to find all this information?"

In five minutes, we find a bunch of articles from economic journals on the industry that I'm interested in…all on the Internet of course. Impressive!

I'm feeling so good about my shift that I actually decided to accept invitations from Gideon should he be so bold as to make them. Since Daichi, I haven't been accepting invitations, certainly not from Americans, but I was feeling so mellow what with the sense of power and control I was getting over my own money. Why not? What could a small outing with a neighbor hurt?

Like Tracy Chapman says, "If not now what then/We all must live our lives/Always feeling/Always thinking/The moment has arrived."

(He loaned me a couple of albums...)

Massage Session #8

Dan: Good afternoon, Ms. Gold. How is your research coming along?

Franny: Well, copper IUDs are distributed most widely in China, 73.5 percent, and the least in sub-Saharan Africa, .05 percent. I'm investigating the methods used in China and discovering if there is any company willing to expand operations into other parts of the world with a similar model. I know it's a long shot, and I think that those can be the ones that really pan out. What do you think?

Dan: I agree with you. That kind of precision judgment is very error-prone, but the timing is easier. You already know you're early. The only question is are you really helping people get what they want.

Franny: You're scaring me!

Dan: Ms. Gold, if you feel safe investing your money like that, you don't understand the game you're in. I'll tell you how I handle the fear. In tough market cycles like the one we're in today, I keep most of my money invested safely, and I only speculate with a little of it, maybe thirty or forty percent at risk.

I'm saving most of my risk-taking for the easy pickings – the low-risk entry point that I'm looking for in late 2006 or 2007. Because I've been so careful during the tough times, I'll have plenty of money available to buy great stocks from panicked investors who are deserting the market like rats deserting a sinking ship at just the wrong time.

I think the herd will be overreacting as the economy goes through its normal slowing phase. That slowing will be totally normal for the healthiest economy in the world to go through at this time in the cycle, just like it's normal for our healthy planet to go through winter. It gets cold and the vegetables die, but it doesn't mean we're facing destruction. With no sense of history or timing, though, the herd will overreact as usual, and I'll be right there to benefit.

Franny: I still don't get what you mean by the cycle.

Dan: I'm showing you what it looks like when it's a good time for bonds and how this will be inevitably followed by a low-risk/high-reward time for moving back to the stock market. I want you to understand this and be as confident about it as you are confident that spring will follow winter.

In winter, your job is to hold on and make it through. It's a waste of your time and energy to desperately try to plant your vegetables in the winter. Spring is the time for planting and opportunity. Market cycles are just as easy to understand once you know what you're looking for.

Franny: Once you know what you're looking for... You know, this is starting to make sense. My next question is, "Should I be worried?"

Dan: It does make sense, and yes, I guess you should be worried.

Anyway, let me take you through the economic winter. Right around 2001, I realized that the world has changed...again. All of these new companies have been created. They've been created by Asians moving from the country to the city and becoming middle-class. They've been created by Africans and Latin Americans. All of these people want to be in business, and they all want to compete with the American companies that your stock broker and mutual fund guy are pushing.

All of these new people around the world want to work cheaper, and they have similar skills, similar patents and intellectual property. So it isn't easy for the old winner companies to make a lot of money, right now. And remember: Those public companies have to make enough to pay huge salaries to their top executives before they share any of the profits with you.

Here's how I responded. With all these people wanting to get into business, what's the one thing they don't have? Capital. We in the Western, industrial world are the only ones who have capital,

130

because a hundred years ago we were already creating a surplus of savings when they were out there in the fields planting rice. To be in business, everybody has to scramble for the scarce capital, and I'm lucky enough to have some. Why do I want to be a company competing and knocking my head against the wall? Why don't I be a lender that they have to pay first?

Today, with my investments mostly in bonds, I'm making eight or nine percent interest on my money. It's not thirty percent, but even aggressive most stock investors aren't making thirty percent anyway, these days.

[To delve deeper into the bonds The Moneyman is talking about, go to http://www.escapefromtheherd.com and download a special audio report.]

Sure, I'd like to make thirty percent on the stock market, but if I have to bang my head against the wall to make something between ten and thirty, like most investors are, why don't I just lend the guy money and make good money while I sleep like a baby on 400 thread-per-inch sheets, right? So, what I realized in 2001 is: If I can help people double their money safely every seven, eight or even ten years in this kind of environment, I'm going to be a real hero. I know how it's going to come out. I'll sleep at night, and I'll wait for the easy entry point to make the big money in the stock market.

That's why I started to put a lot of money into special issue bonds. And you know what? All that safety took a lot of the pressure off of me and even made me a better stock investor, with my little bit of risk capital. I see all those overcommitted, wildly emotional people who have all their money at risk in stocks. They're living in hope and dying in despair. With a lot of money invested safely, I feel like Cool Hand Luke.

Franny: Cool Hand Luke. That's an interesting expression. I'm going to look up its origin when I get home. But, yes, I do hear you, Dan. You found the perfect place to invest during this wintery spell.

Dan: I like to think so. When I was thinking about how tough the stock market was getting back in 2001, I knew guys on Wall Street who had gone the other way and were involved in the bond business. I didn't know anything about bonds. I hadn't bought a bond since my nephew's bar mitzvah. I was interested in the cool stuff, but I realized very few people were going to make any money in stocks. It was just too tough. So I went and found a way to lend money so that I could be the guy on the outside of the fray.

It's analogous to this scenario: There's this gold field and all the people want to go in and find gold. There's only a little gold and endless people pouring in to find it. They're killing each other. I'd rather be the guy on the edge of the field selling shovels. The truth is most of them are not going to find enough gold to pay for their shovel. I'm selling capital.

Franny: So, maybe I should get a little off the path of the middle-class herd and look at what the big guys do with their money and only play with a portion of what I have.

Dan: Exactly. The only reason I'm happy in tough times is because I'm much more successful when my whole life doesn't depend on every deal. I'm more successful and happy when most of my money is collecting an interest check every month. That's why I'm better at investing in stocks than other people are. They're over-committed and sweating it, and I'm not.

Franny: Not to be argumentative, Dan, but in general how am I supposed to know what the big guys do with their money? It's not like a column in *Bust Magazine* or on right after the *Home Makeover Edition* show.

Dan: Good question.

Franny: On a different subject, did you do your yoga?

Dan: Actually, Ms. Gold, it's not an entirely different subject. As you've had me doing so much yoga lately, I've realized that I've been doing a kind of yoga all along, just investment yoga.

Franny: Say again?

Dan: One way I keep from becoming a member of the herd is by not over-committing. "Play within yourself" they call it in sports. In other words, that basketball player, he's playing within himself. He's playing his own game; he's not trying to be Michael Jordan. He's doing what he knows how to do, and he's winning. The strategy in a match would be to pull him out of his game.

In general it's important for me to keep myself feeling like it's all just a walk in the park. One of the things I do as a model for how to set goals is I know when I have too much emotion in-vested in something because it creates adrenaline. I know, just like a golfer, I cannot play on adrenaline. What we're doing requires too much fine discrimination and skills to do it when you're on adrenaline. When you have a lot of emotion invested in something, it stimulates endocrine secretions, which make it very difficult for you to behave as the smart, successful you. You become the impulsive foolish you – there's one of those in each of us. That's what human beings are. And what I do is I know what it feels like to be hyped on adrenaline and I consciously step away when I feel that way.

You see, I may have as a goal that I want to get my kids into college. I may have as a goal that I want to look good. I may have a goal that I want to be loved by the people around me. Well, when I start making goals like that, not getting them is *very scary*. A lot of times, you feel good talking about your goals. When it comes time to play the game and you're focusing on those goals, it's all adrenaline. It's like you're in the World Series, and you're in the last out. Very few people perform well in those types of situations.

On the other hand, if I can think in terms of how important it is for me to get a better tennis serve, and I wish my desk was waxed better, then I'm relaxed. There's this new style of shirt I was thinking I would get. If I can make these things my goals, I can be as calm in the big situation as Joe Montana, the Hall-of-Fame quarterback. Joe Montana could be in the Super Bowl and it felt like he was shopping for a pair of socks because he knew how to stay in the right mental zone. That's why he was paid twelve million dollars a year. You have to feel like it's just a walk in the park, like you're having a day off. You can't feel like you're playing for all the marbles. That's a very important thing. When I am too upset, I walk away.

Again, I'm liberated by the fact that there's always another deal.

My grandfather told me this when I was a kid, and it's still just as true today. Remember this idea, and it alone will put you in the top ten percent of investors. I always remember that there's never been a deal that I can't walk away from, mainly because another deal always comes along very soon. Money is scarce; deals are not. If I'm not totally in the right zone, I don't want to play. *Remember, I have to have the total advantage.* If I'm starting to lose the advantage because I'm starting to play too hard, starting to get adrenaline rush, I walk away. I simply will not play when I am nervous, upset, worried or anything else. A lot of times, I can go do a meditation and think about buying a better pair of socks and think about those kinds of things.

Franny: A better pair of socks?

Dan: You know, something trivial and non-stressful.

Franny: Oh, that's like what I do when I remember *I Love Lucy* episodes.

Dan: Yes, like that. Another thing I do is control my environment. If you're around chocolate all day, you might get sick of it but chances are that wouldn't happen until you gained about ten pounds. I believe in putting myself in a physical space that is conducive to detached, careful thought.

You'd notice that if you come to my office. It's a different type of environment. You go into a lot of investment offices, and you expect to see Bloomberg machines and clocks on the wall and young people running back and forth. Instead, I'm in a place in the sky that's surrounded by windows, and I'm looking out the window. Everything out there looks like it's moving in slow motion. I work in a place like this so I can remember that, despite what they're telling me on television, everything looks pretty much the same as it did yesterday and as it did last week, last month, a hundred years ago, or a thousand years ago. Our lives are full of frenetic change, but Planet Earth stays pretty much the same. Whatever just happened in the news is really not as earth-shaking as they make it seem on TV. In this way, I keep myself in context. I'm good at this because I make these decisions in my ivory tower, not on the floor of the NYMEX or the NYSE.

Franny: That is exactly why I painted my room and all my furniture white. I have white sheets and blankets, and the floor is white. Everything except a huge framed square of blue over the bed is white. I just needed to feel like I was on the beach. Lately, though, my feng shui friend told me that I need a picture of two things together to create a context of love and friendship. I got two shells and a jar of sand. That should do it. When I'm at the beach, I mean in my bedroom, I just listen to my wave CD. It's very peaceful.

Gideon says that we are the wave, and God is the ocean. He meditates quite a lot in order to merge with the ocean. We have that in common: I mean a love of the ocean.

Dan: There's environment, and I've also got a built-in support system. I've got guys who know way more about this than your stock broker does, and they are my committee that helps me all the time.

But in the end, we are all totally alone. We die alone, and at the moment of truth, we are alone. I am absolutely bound and determined. I'm not going to lose because of my closest advisors, my wife, my friends or my stock broker. I may lose, but it will be because I got it wrong. I'm not going down because of somebody else. No one can take responsibility but me, so I always make the call. No matter how big I get, I will always make the call, and no matter how small you are, you need to always make the call. That would have saved you from that stupid mistake in March 2000. No offense.

Franny: No offense taken.

Dan: Another thing is that I have to get into what I call context. I have to remember where I am. I'm not landing on the beach of Normandy. I have time, but I have to understand what it is I am doing.

The first thing I have to do is manually disconnect myself from the herd, manually pull the plug and say, "OK. I am no longer a herd animal." When I hear the little voice saying, "It's going to go away. You're wife's going to think you're stupid. Your wife's going to know you lost money," I realize that I'm not disconnected from the herd.

I begin to disconnect. Maybe I'll do a little meditation and I'll think of myself as a flower and I'll think of all those people around me and I feel the stress dissolving between me and them. As I do that I feel that I'm a flower and it's just me in the sun and I feel myself getting stronger and stronger. I do that all the time.

Franny: Yes. You do it so gently. I'm more like "snap the twig." I'm more like "Franny, get over it!" It's the same thing; just one is gentle and the other one is a quick pop. Did your mom ever whip you with one of those wooden paddles with a little red ball on the end? Mine would just whack me once. That's what I do; I give myself a stinging whack.

Dan: I've noticed that you're a little hard on yourself, Ms. Gold. I used to be very hard on myself. There was a guy…A manager of mine when I was working as a financial salesman sat in on a sale I was making to a client, and just as the client was about to seal the sale, this manager interrupted and basically changed the client's mind by just talking too much. My manager realized that he blew the deal. We went to the car, and he says to me, "You know I'm really sorry. I should have known better than to open my mouth."

And I said to him, "You know, these things happen. Don't give it a thought. You're a wonderful guy, don't sweat it." Then I realized how I talk to myself when I blow one compared to how I talked to him. I decided that I'm going to treat myself as well as I treat that jerk.

Today when I make a mistake, I stop berating myself, hating myself and killing myself, making it so painful that I'm afraid to make another mistake. Instead of being a pin-cushion or a punching bag, I treat myself like the winner that I am. I allow myself to have errors, and I look at the whole context.

By the way, Ms. Gold, one of the reasons I'm taking the time to talk to you and tell you all of this is that I used to be one of these middlemen. I was a hired gun so I really do know what I'm talking about.

Franny: You sold insurance and annuities and were making money on warehousing?

Dan: Yes, as a young man that is exactly what I did until I wised up. Anyway, let's continue on, shall we? Yes, we want to give ourselves a break when we make mistakes.

We keep coming back to the fact that this is not about us and how much love we deserve. What is our main goal, the reason we can invest and make money in the first place? What are we doing? We're helping the world get what it wants. We're helping hundreds, thousands and millions of people get what they want. Overall, people are better off because of us. We make mistakes, but as long as we're honest about it, we can make sure the world is better off with us than without us. You see, I remember where I am and who I am. This quiet, calm environment helps me do that.

140

When the average investor makes a mistake, she thinks the mistake is about technical analysis or reported earnings, or the government. The truth is, nine out of ten times, it's really about the **mental game**.

Some people are so ego-involved they're willing to pay to be right. They've been trained to believe errors are horrible and humiliating. It's almost as if guys feel they have smaller testicles when they make mistakes. Making mistakes in the market is like having small wheels on your pickup truck. It's all tied up with their machismo. They don't want to believe their wife could be better at it. You can fill in the equivalent ego-driven error for women, but any way you slice it, all of this is still just another version of being ruled by the herd. I think of it like this, this is why I can tolerate mistakes – because I treat everything that I do as simply an opportunity for correction. My job is not to rate myself. In fact, I do my best to avoid rating myself at all. Sometimes I have to catch myself, but I'm working on this all the time.

First I'm simply God's child. I deserve love regardless of my performance.

Secondly, everything I do is an opportunity for correction. I never think of anything I do as correct because I think everything can always get a little better. My process is simple; I simply do something and then correct mistakes. Every trade or deal I do is an opportunity for correction. It's a probe of the world to see what's working and what's not working. I don't go in there grading myself as a success or failure. I go in there thinking, "What will I need to do to correct this?"

I want to see what the error is so I can correct it and get it better. I'm thinking like a general.

Imagine a general who's in the Vietnam War. He's got 3,000 troops with him in the jungle, and he knows there are thousands of enemy out there in the jungle and he doesn't know where they are. He's got to find out where they are to keep his men alive. He's got to probe. That's how I am with the market. I'm not exactly sure how the market is going to behave every time. I have to probe and see.

The General can't see where the enemy troops are. They're just out there in the jungle. He says to the sergeant, "Have one guy go out 100 yards, turn around and come back. Do not fight. Avoid the enemy. Just see if you can see him and then come back."

Then he sends another guy out 1 degree the other way, and he might start sending guys out over there out 200 yards. You've got to know where the enemy is. Eventually, one of these guys is going to encounter the enemy and possibly get killed. The General's got thousands of people whose lives he has to preserve, and he's got to find out where the enemy is. Killing one or two of his guys is not pleasant, but it is impossible for him to do his job without killing some soldiers. That's why they're there, right?

This General is playing for higher stakes than I am, much higher. It doesn't matter because, in his game or in ours, if you can't pull the trigger, you can't be the General. We need a General who can do this. He'll keep probing and sending his men out as thoughtfully and carefully as he can. When he sends them out and loses a couple of guys, he learns where the enemy is. This way he keeps most of the thousands of troops alive.

Now here's the part that will help you understand this game and be a better player!

No doubt, to the dead guy's family, the General's actions were a mistake. That's their point of view. To him, it's a probe. That's how I feel about my transactions. Nothing can be done without losing some men, or in my case, some money. Every encounter can bring some kind of loss... I'm not trying to avoid mistakes; I'm trying to avoid big losses by identifying small losses.

Franny: War metaphors again. You know, when I'm rolling in dough, one of the things I'm going to do is start a non-violent problem-solving institute. It will be very prestigious and hard to get into. The only way you can get in is to show an imaginative way to win World War II without using deadly force. Personally,

I have figured it out using potatoes. You may laugh, but if you look at the difference between Einstein and every other mathematician, it was that he used his imagination.

I'm glad you're getting something out of your yoga. I want you to use the ball a little bit, too. Marcel will show you how. Just do it when you come to the club, and that's going to help with the strength in those abdominal and quadratus luborum, your lower back.

Dan: See you next week. Have a good weekend.

Points

- Practice some form of meditation frequently to go within and remove your connection to the stressors around you. By the way, many Americans call this prayer. For our purposes, it makes no difference at all.

- Use a kind of "mind yoga" to keep your thinking calm and removed from the herd. Instead of thinking of your decisions as life or death matters, put them into the perspective of small, everyday decisions, like picking out a pair of socks. This allows your mind to move away from the threat of adrenaline.

- Create a peaceful removed environment where you can maintain the context of perspective.

- Establish a good support group of other people who know the market and who also keep themselves away from the herd.

- Treat yourself like the winner that you are. Allow yourself to have errors; look at the whole context.

- **Everything you do is an opportunity for correction. Don't think of anything you do as correct because everything can always get a little better.**

- **Simply do something and then correct mistakes. When you learn to do this without rating yourself, you'll already be getting richer and your investments will already be making you more money.**

- **Do not try to avoid mistakes; try to avoid big losses by identifying small losses.**

- **Do not allow yourself to be sucked into taking more risk than you can handle emotionally. In other words, LIQUIDATE TO THE SLEEPING POINT!**

Franny's Thoughts

It's been over a week since I decided to accept invitations from Gideon, and yet he has not been ready with one. I wonder if I should let him know that this golden window of opportunity may soon close. Nah. Well, maybe just a hint like I'll ask him if he's tried the new Mongolian barbeque place or maybe what kind of food they eat in Malibu. Yeah. I would like to know that. I'm thinking very expensive avocado dishes. I've never actually wanted to go to Malibu. I imagine it's a lot of set people and people who do commercials hanging out at swank coffee shops talking movies, wearing a glove on one arm or fedoras.

It turns out that I don't see Gideon all weekend. I don't care. I'm very busy doing my research, and I went to a Burundian Independence Day party. I called and told my guy at American Express to sell all my shares in my mutual fund. He told me that I'm crazy basically. I was so cheerful with him. The thing is now I have to find a new financial guy I think, or maybe not. I don't have to know my next move in order to stop doing something I know is wrong, do I?

Being master of my own destiny is actually a huge side benefit of all this. I am so shifted. I actually priced flights to New Zealand. Just between you and me, I've always wanted a skinny man to sashay around and clean my house. Standard uniform, but if he could also do the lawn, I would be in heaven. That is one thing about people from other countries, at least those from developing or fundamentalist countries; they don't naturally make you breakfast in bed, not to mention cleaning. No, those are definitely rare but existing traits of the American man.

Finally, I just sort of dropped by Gideon's place to tell him about my decision to go with a dual condom/ IUD distributor in Thailand. He was home (I saw his car there), but he didn't answer the door. I found that irritating. (Franny Gold does not knock on doors when the person is home and they don't answer without closing her window of opportunity.)

Massage Session #9

Franny: Dan, Dan The Moneyman invested one and he made ten, Dan, Dan The Moneyman.

Dan: Not bad.

Franny: Hey, I've got a question for you. I went and dumped all my mutual funds. Now I'm wondering if I need to find a new guy. I don't have much money, but my guy is like one of those con-men you were talking about.

Dan: Since you don't want to get conned, but you do want to invest in the stock market, I suggest you get a discount stock broker in which the transaction costs are near zero. Then I think you should seek out whatever you need elsewhere. I do not believe you should seek guidance or information from a stock broker. There's very little chance they'll have anything but con-flicted interests and incorrect information. Number one: we discussed earlier that stock brokers have no training in how to make money for anybody but the companies they work for. Their training is in sales, not in investment. One of the interesting pieces of evidence is that if your stock broker was on the level, she would be consulted by her company at the time when that company is deploying its capital.

Another question to ask yourself is what happens when your

stock broker fails in business or gets fired? Does he go to work at the top of the Empire State Building for another investment bank, or does he go out and get a job selling siding somewhere?

In my opinion, it's number two. He's a salesman. I would say that in this day and age, because of the spread of technology and computers, you don't require a middleman to assist you in purchasing securities. You can do it without any assistance from him, and you can do it for pennies a share. There's no reason to have a middleman like that. On the other hand, you should seek out as much information as you can get, and you should use sources that don't get paid commission for selling you something.

Anybody who has any amount of money sophistication understands conflicts of interest. They don't get into deals where they have to trust people who have clear conflicts of interest. Let me give you some examples of how the question "How do I identify a stock broker?" manifests itself. Here's one really good example.

Bear in mind, Ms. Gold, that the word fiduciary means "in a special position of trust." The Securities and Exchange Commission, a government agency, regulates fiduciary advisors. The National Association of Securities Dealers, a self-regulating organization, regulates stock brokers and insurance agents.

Because an advisor presents himself as being in a special position of trust, SEC regulations require first that an advisor be acting on your behalf when he's receiving fees from you.

If there are conflicts of interest, such as your trusted advisor, he is required to disclose them clearly. That's the law.

Stock brokerage firms are agents representing people who want to raise money by selling you shares. Investors or customers are expected to be aware that the agent or broker is not on their side and is receiving commissions from the other team – the sellers. Brokers used to be right out in the open but are trying to camouflage themselves these days. The public is pretty much on to them. So they're trying to camouflage themselves by calling themselves "advisors." They are setting up one-price systems and different wrap systems that appear to be advisory when, in fact, the brokers are the same wolves they always were. These firms have secured, through heavy lobbying, a variance or an exception from the SEC. Because of who they are, big brokerage firms, they're allowed to use the word *advisor* for which they're using all kinds of novel spellings. They're the only ones right now who are allowed to call themselves advisors and not disclose conflicts of interest.

This is not an accident! These large brokerage firms have the bald-faced nerve to go and specifically write arguments about why it would be bad for them to disclose conflicts of interest. I can't imagine it. If you read it in law school, I'm sure it would be a classic for debating.

I can't think of one possible good reason why someone should be allowed to call himself an advisor and not have to disclose conflicts of interest. I'm not saying relationships don't occasionally produce conflicts of interest. I'm just saying he ought to be responsible enough to disclose those conflicts when he presents himself as an advisor or fiduciary. Somehow, through nefarious means, brokers have secured exception that allows them to call themselves advisors but spell it funny and not disclose conflicts of interest. If this doesn't tell you that you ought to run the other way, I don't know what will.

Franny: Those are strong words.

Dan: I don't want to get my information and decision-making data from someone who makes a profit on my purchase. Number two: I don't want to get financial advice from somebody who has less money than I do and doesn't have a clue. Number three: I don't want to use sponsored information, but if that's all I can get, I'm going to be extra careful and extra skeptical. Therefore, the only thing left is that I have to spend a few dollars to get good information. Now, I will leave it to you to decide what that is.

Franny: Thanks. You're very clear. I'll think about it and discuss it with my partner.

Dan: You have a partner?

Franny: Well, Gideon, my neighbor, has been working with me on the research. He's like a partner, in a way.

Dan: It's good that you are working as a team. When you start out, the small print can be daunting, but don't let it stop you. There's a great deal of money to be made if you will stick with it.

Instead of going on free Internet sites like Yahoo and screening for the P/E ratio, which is total nonsense, look up specific companies. If I wanted to make a 10,000 dollar investment, and I wanted to get good at this, one of the things I might do is make a disproportionately expensive trip to the company in which I was thinking of investing. I would do this because not only do I have to take a vacation once in a while, but I'm going to learn about something to invest in. Above all, I'm making an investment in my abilities that transcends the amount of money I'm investing in the company. The question is, "Are you really willing to do what it takes to get good at this?" If you're not, pay somebody to do it well. "Pay someone good to do it" translates to "pay someone a high salary to do it." Unless you want to spend your money this way, it is far better to do the research yourself. That way, you can call the shots.

My friend, who is a writer, writes infomercials. He told me about his experience with the Cathy Smith infomercial: How Cathy

Smith, through the magic of her skills, helps you look better, feel better, lose weight and be healthy. Cathy Smith is a very attractive person and quite knowledgeable, and they make nice infomercials. Unfortunately, her company just about breaks even by the time they pay themselves for doing the work. Cathy Smith tells you the magic of following her advice, but somewhere in there she tells you that you'll have to stop eating everything in sight and a certain amount of exercise will be required.

No matter how easy she makes it look, she can't compete with Richard Simmons, who makes a million dollars a day with infomercials that say, "Deal-a-Meal just allows you to take a card from this side and move it over to the other side and dance around with some nice-looking people of whatever gender you prefer, and the pounds just melt away, and you'll look great." Deal-a-Meal sells much more than Cathy Smith does, because people prefer to be in a world in which they can lose weight easily with Deal-a-Meal. If I'm willing to suspend that one simple requirement – telling the truth – I can sell anything to the gullible public.

I'm constantly amazed that people believe it takes twenty years of practice to solder a pipe, that it requires all kinds of apprenticeship. They scoff at the idea that someone could read a book and do it because there are so many variables and eventualities that occur in soldering a pipe. It really takes so much experience before you're any good at it.

Then, they absolutely believe that it takes years and years to learn how to do surgery on somebody's brain. Yet, by far, the best paying job is making money in the markets. Do you think that those who make money this way have years of experience and skills doing it? They do.

There are only a few people who professionally manage and invest money successfully, and they all make a fortune. Yet, for some reason, the general public has it in their mind that they can go to a seminar or read a newspaper and compete with people who have been competing on Wall Street all their lives. I think there's an amazing amount of self-delusion involved in that kind of belief. You understand why I tell that story in advance of telling you the truth? It's because I know what you want to hear.

Franny: I might just have to take a trip to Thailand. I hear the beaches there are spectacular and that HIV and AIDS is rampant.

Dan: That's what I hear, too. They are probably the best place to find business discussions on the effective distribution of condoms and birth control. Good call.

Franny: Yeah, it is, isn't it? I'm getting the hang of this stuff.

Dan: You are getting the hang of it, Ms. Gold. Just stay focused and do your own work. I don't mean to be a wet blanket, but I just want you to understand how much information and advantage the other guys have in comparison. When you get the idea that you cannot compete in the same leagues with the big guys, you will stop relying on false information, stop trying to outsmart the world, and stop trying to come up with easy technical gimmicks or software. Forget about the silver bullets. Come up with a plan that you're able to do well, then just play within yourself. You don't have to make more baskets than Michael Jordan. You just have to get the ball in the hole a few times to have a very lovely and affluent life.

Franny: Fine. I'll play within myself, but I'm finding this really interesting now. Just out of curiosity, how does a guy who's been at it all his life do it?

Dan: The psychological aspects of investing in the stock market are just as important to me as any other part – actually more important. The market may be great, but if people don't feel like buying stocks, then the market is still going to go down. This is where I part company with a lot of "experts." A lot of people say, "This looks good, and so and so company is going to make money. The stock should be going up, and I'm going to invest in it."

Then they're disappointed because they didn't see that ninety percent of the people aren't in the mood to buy stocks for whatever reason. I spend a lot of time on measuring what people are feeling, because if everybody is feeling awful about stocks, it doesn't matter how good things are at a particular company. That's why a lot of my work is focused on what *is* happening rather than what *should be* happening.

I want to know if people are buying stocks and how enthusiastically they are buying them. I also want to know whether they are offering stocks for sale, taking profits or exiting in panic.

One good indicator was invented by a trader, Karl Eggerss. Karl knows people buy certain kinds of options to protect their portfolios from losing value when stocks are being sold. Without going into too much boring detail, investors buy options that give them the right, but not the obligation, to sell their holdings at specific market prices. That way if the stocks fall in price, they're protected. They have bought the right to sell at the previous higher price. They used to call this "portfolio insurance."

The people who buy options tend to be the most emotional and impulsive of investors, and they tend to be wrong at key turning points. When they start getting scared, they buy more put options and they drive up the option prices or premiums.

Karl learned to study the price movements of a basket of options, to infer how scared or happy the crazy, impulsive investors were getting at a certain moment in time. The more panic investors feel, the higher Karl's Crazy Investor Indicator goes.

Because they tend to be most panicky at the bottom and most happy at the top, he learned to use this indicator to find low-risk moments when it is safer to buy in a temporary lull in a bull market, and to find the right moment of excessive euphoria to sell in a bear market.

When Karl's Crazy Investor Indicator is soaring, it shows that these most emotional investors are panicky. As you can imagine, that's often a good time to buy because investors are generally tossing stocks out the window and prices go down rather dramatically. They often overdo this selling, and so stock prices sometimes get very attractive before they start to come back. This works great in a bull market because investors who panic during a bull market are wrong.

In a bear or down stock market, everything changes and the Crazy Investors tell us when it's an opportune time to sell. If stock prices are rising temporarily, the news media are generally reporting happy economic news and those crazy options buyers begin to feel euphoric. The happier and more confident they are, the more they want to buy stocks, and that demand drives the prices higher. They also feel so confident, they feel they don't need to protect themselves by buying portfolio insurance, so the prices of those put options decline. Those are euphoric times when stock prices are peaking, and they present an opportunity to sell at an advantageous moment for top dollar.

Franny: You just buy when they're scared and sell whenever you see them get happy? I thought you don't believe in silver bullets.

Dan: Right. There aren't any. I'm afraid getting rich is never that simple. Otherwise, there would be a lot more rich people. Here's the problem.

Many teenagers think society is always wrong, but that just isn't true. The crowd isn't always wrong. Following the crowd, or always doing the opposite of the crowd – both those habits are equally dangerous. Let me give you an example:

You remember back in the late nineties, when the technology stocks were running. We've talked about that time before. During that long bull market, being happy as an investor wasn't wrong. A lot of technical traders in the media used to keep telling people to sell because the market was "complacent." In a bull market like we were in, investors who were happy weren't wrong, Ms. Gold, and the wise guys who bet on stocks falling when investors were too happy got buried. Most of them are driving cabs now. Karl's Crazy Investor Indicator can be lethal if you read it wrong. As you said, there really are no silver bullets.

By the same token, in 2001, we were in the early stages of a multi-year bear market during which prices of the ex-big winners fell by seventy percent or even ninety percent. Believe me, I've seen my share of bear markets.

Maybe you can remember when tech stock prices first started to fall. As they usually do in the first stage of the bear market, prices dropped quickly by about twenty percent. Those same money-losing experts told people that investor panic was a buying opportunity. But in a bear market, scared investors aren't wrong or crazy. Those who swooped in and bought the dips got murdered. Once again, the Crazy Investors can kill you if you don't stay awake!

Franny: I see. So the sellers are right in a bear market, and the buyers are right in a bull market. Just one question: how do I know which one we're in, Dan?

Dan: That's where the art comes in. Actually, when we're in the middle of one of these directional markets, it's pretty easy. You can feel the momentum. But at the turning points, it is pretty dicey. It takes a lot of practice, and nobody can get it right all the time. But if you stay awake, consider every move an opportunity for correction, you'll eventually get a feel for the rhythm of the market.

Having a feeling about what you're looking for helps. Remember the other day I told you about the major buying opportunity I'm looking for in late 2006 or early 2007, following a huge round of panic and fear? You see, when I know what I'm looking for, the Crazy Investors can help me find the right moment to make my move.

By spring 2000, we were used to making great money by buying whenever we saw the herd panicking. It was called "Buying the Dips" and lots of people were making a fortune at it, but all of a sudden, buying on panic stopped being profitable. The Crazy Investor Indicator showed that investors were frightened, but when we bought the stocks, we just didn't make money.

I wish I could tell you that I picked up on the change right away, but after all those years of bull market and making a fortune on every dip, it took a while to wake up. It wasn't the first time I'd fallen asleep and was slow waking up. Fortunately, I finally caught on and that's when I reached some of the conclusions we talked about earlier about how tough the stock market was going to get.

That bear market lasted until March 2003, and investors who never caught on and continued doing what they were doing before lost a pile of dough – about three TRILLION dollars. That's trillion with a T. Whether it's 1,000 or one trillion, to me it's all about the game.

We were used to making money by selling every time investors got too happy or enthusiastic. But all of a sudden, selling when Karl's Crazy Investor Indicator hit bottom just stopped working – just like that! That spring, the world ran out of stock sellers. Some brave people started to buy stocks, and prices started to rise a little. Our old trick of selling when they got happy didn't work that time.

Actually, I remember the exact moment in March 2003 when the stock market turned and the bear died. I woke at two a.m. on a Saturday night for some reason and couldn't sleep, so I turned on Fox News. The United States had attacked Saddam Hussein, and emotions were running very high. The Fed had been dropping money out of helicopters for a while already, but there was, so far, no sign of the economy picking up.

Anyway, the TV had all these old generals saying that our soldiers were "bogged down" and there weren't enough "boots on the ground."

Franny: I remember those generals. Whatever happened to them? I think they disappeared.

Dan: Probably. But the thing that really got me was this ten-minute report they gave at two a.m. It was about these people in Vermont, in the snow, wrapping their house with plastic and duct tape. I laughed so loud and hard as I watched this story I woke up my wife. Together we lay there roaring with laughter. I guess the people in the story were trying to avoid being gassed by terror-ists, but we couldn't figure out whether they meant to be inside the plastic or outside. I told my wife, "This has to be the bottom. I'm going to start buying stocks." Monday morning I bought about forty million dollars worth of stocks, and I kept buying all week.

That moment marked a major turning point. Fortunately, it didn't take me a year to catch on that time. I had learned my lesson and wasn't feeling overconfident. You see, Ms. Gold, if you're alert at those times and not overly confident, you can see that something has changed. Selling when investors act happy stopped making us money, so we considered that maybe we weren't in a bear market anymore. Fortunately, we were early and had a terrific couple of years buying on fear again.

Franny: It's like you've lived several lives already.

Dan: You could say that. Actually, another change occurred in 2004. Wall Street entered a kind of in-between sideways stage, which is where we are today. To make good money at a time like this, you really have to buy when the herd panics and sell when it gets too happy.

It isn't that easy. You have to be wide awake all the time and absolutely free yourself of your own beliefs and the beliefs of all the "experts" around you. That's not so easy to do, either, because those experts sound really smart and convincing. This is what I meant the other day when we talked about discipline over conviction.

When the herd is scared, it thinks the economy is falling off the cliff. When all we hear are worries about interest rates, deficits, the Fed, oil, war and that the country is falling into a recession, it's hard not to be scared. You don't feel like buying, and the herd animal inside you is screaming to run away with the herd. But that's the moment when you can make the big bucks. In a bull market, the smart money buys when the herd is in panic, and viceversa in a bear market.

See APPENDIX 1 for a more scholarly discussion of the
CRAZY INVESTOR INDICATOR

By the way, Ms. Gold, this or anything else could change at any moment. But I usually try to keep somewhere in my mind, the fact that betting against the United States – its economy, its ingenuity, its army – has, so far, proven to be the worst bet on the planet over the past 200-plus years.

Franny: Whew! I guess you've been told that when you get going on a subject, you're like a force of nature.

Dan: Yes, I've heard that.

Franny: I get the gist of what you're saying, but I'm going to have to experience some of it myself to really understand.

Dan: Yes, it's like speaking a language. You just have to do it and then it makes sense.

Franny: Hmm. You've given me a lot to think about Dan The Moneyman. I'll see you next time!

Dan: See you next time.

Points

- Be very wary of the advice of a stockbroker. They are often conflicted and unreliable.

- Do your own research and use a discount brokerage account to process your own trades. Seek out as much information as you can get and use sources that don't get paid commission for selling you something.

- Stock brokerage firms are agents representing people who want to raise money by selling you shares. Investors or customers are expected to be aware that the agent or broker is not on their side and is receiving commissions from the other team – the sellers. Conflicts of interest abound, but brokers do not always disclose them to you.

- When you get the idea that you cannot compete in the same leagues with the big guys, you will stop relying on false information, stop trying to outsmart the world, and stop trying to come up with easy technical gimmicks or software. Forget about the silver bullets. Come up with a plan that you're able to do well, then just play within yourself.

- At the turning points in a bear or bull market, it's hard to tell what direction the market will take. It takes a lot of practice, and nobody can get it right all the time.

- Understanding the cycles helps you watch for major turning points, which almost always bring with them huge opportunities.

- In a bull market, you should be seeking to buy at moments of greatest fear and panic.

- In a bear market, you should seek to sell at moments of euphoria or complacency.

- Do not rely on your mood or the mood you get from the news media to set your strategy. Develop objective ways of identifying key turning points. The indicators described here are only the beginning. There are hundreds of valid ways to do this. You have to learn to use the ones that are easiest for you to work with. The key is knowing what you are looking for.

- In addition to my work, some of the most valuable work on identifying turning points in herd behavior is done by John Murphy, John Bollinger, Tobin

Smith, Paul Desmond and Helene Meisler. A list of links to these brilliant analysts can be found on www.escapefromtheherd.com .

Franny and Gideon

I'm talking to Gideon about the bulls and the bears and the crazy investors and Dan's many financial lifetimes, and he says to me, "Franny, have you ever noticed how much like love investing is?"

I have to stop right here and tell you that my Dynasty Son Syndrome antennae really went up when I heard that. Why? Because it's *charming.* When a man begins musing about love with a woman, a woman he hasn't slept with, that's called being charming and add being a prince of a sort to it and you've got the most dangerous thing of all, Prince Charming: an illusion to be sure. I've never met a real one; let's put it that way.

Just to see where he was going, I played along with it.

"What do you mean?"

"I mean," he says, giving me the shiny big eye again, "that our money is so close to us. It represents our masculinity, our intelligence, our superiority and a bunch of other stuff. When we risk it on something we believe in or like or have chosen rationally, we're doing the equivalent of opening our hearts up to another person."

"I see." There followed a long pause. "So, have you had a lot of experience investing?"

"Yes and no. I have definitely taken some risks, and I've lost and won, too. So, I've had those experiences. I haven't invested a lot, though." He stopped talking. I didn't say anything. Then he added, "I definitely think it's something I want to do more of. I don't mind losing because I'm going to be a winner in the end if I keep investing wisely."

"A winner." I looked at him. "So, a winner in investing – I know what that looks like. That looks like someone rolling in dough. What does a winner in *love* look like?"

"The market can only be understood over time. Time, Franny, reveals to us the face of the herd and it shows us ourselves in the face of our beloved."

"That's heavy." At this point, I have to tell you, I feel separated from my body. I feel as if I am floating over my own head. In my entire life, I have never heard a man use the word "beloved" in a conversation with me. I once heard a preacher use it.

I tried to focus. "Gideon."

"Yes, Franny."

"Have you ever been…Have you ever been in a long-term enduring relationship?"

"Yes, I've committed to two different women in the past."

"What happened, if you don't mind my asking?"

"One developed an unquenchable desire to live in Alaska, and the other one became a nun."

"A nun? Like the Flying Nun?"

"A Buddhist nun."

"Radical."

"It was difficult, but now we're friends and I'm fine."

"You think time and love are related?"

"Yeah. The way I see it, when you tell someone you love them, what you're really saying is 'I *hope* to love you.' Then, as time passes and you remain, your love actually *becomes*. It's like an option to buy or sell, in a way."

He was blowing my mind! All these years of scratching in the dirt for a sign of emotional solvency, and I suddenly walk into the Taj Mahal?

I, Franny Gold, was speechless. I could not speak. I must have looked suspended because he started laughing at me.

"You talk a big talk. You Malibu guys probably go around musing about love all the time."

"No, actually, most of the guys I grew up with were sort of clones of either their fathers or each other. Love wasn't a big topic of conversation. Money was, though. Money, chicks…and cars."

"You're telling me you're different, aren't you?"

"Yes."

"You know what I have to say to that?"

"What?"

"Time will tell."

That's when he went into a Tracy Chapman impersonation. "Can't believe/It's so hard to find someone/To give affection to/ And from whom you can receive/I guess it's just the draw of the cards/In matters of the heart."

Massage Session #10

Franny: Good afternoon!

Dan: Good to see you.

Franny: I see Marcel got you set up. Is anything bothering you today?

Dan: My neck is killing me again.

Franny: OK. Let's work on that. What were we talking about last time, the middleman con artist?

Dan: Yes, I think so. You know, there's always a con artist out there. Today, it's these phony financial advisors. In the 1920s, it was what they used to call "Bucket Shops." Either way, they want you to play, but they don't want you to win.

Franny: I really think it's great to find out there is all this stuff going on above my head. If you listen to the slugs who have been losing my money all these years, you'd think there really isn't that much to know.

Dan: Trust me, Ms. Gold. Lots of people know a lot about this stuff; they just don't tell it to the regular people.

Franny: That's exactly what I want to talk about. See, you've shown me all this stuff about prices going up and prices going down. But everybody knows the markets have been actually going up for hundreds of years. Even I know that stocks are the most profitable investment over the long term. So first of all, why would I want to keep changing things when stocks always go up anyway? If stocks always go up, how come I don't make any money owning them? That seems impossible to me, or am I just that unlucky?

Dan: OK, OK. Look, you can look at things a lot of different ways. Sure, stocks have gone up in the long run over hundreds of years. And, if you were a tree, Ms. Gold, that's probably all you'd have to know because you'd have plenty of time to wait around. But human beings can't afford to spend decades losing money because of some vague beliefs about history. We have to be more precise.

Here's the real history, in a little more useful form, so you can develop a plan that matches your life expectancy that doesn't require hundreds of years to work. We can't just keep playing the market for a hundred and fifty years, can we?

Follow this picture that shows the Dow Industrial Index year-by-year. In fact, each line represents one year on the Dow:

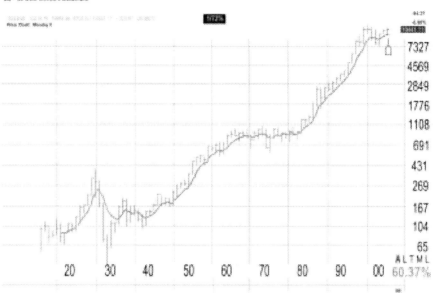

From the 1960s to 1982, the stock market was flat. The Dow Jones Industrials gave us a shorthand way to track the market's action. People who invested in 1964, when the Dow was at 1,000, made nothing over the next eighteen years. In 1982, the Dow was still at 1,000!

If they knew to invest in gold mining at that time, they made a fortune, but then, they made nothing on gold from 1982 all the way until 2001. Any way you look at it, it's still a matter of being in the right place at the right time.

Franny: If I bought good solid stocks and held on to them patiently for eighteen years, I'd have made nothing? That doesn't quite fit with what I've been told before.

Dan: All the way from 1915 in WWI through the Korean War in 1951, stock prices went essentially nowhere. Investors in the Dow Jones Industrials, and the stock market in general, didn't make any money at all for holding onto them. As you can see from this picture, it wasn't that the stock prices stood still. They fluctuated violently and gave investors a very bumpy ride. But after all those years, the stock returns were almost even. However, most investors didn't break even because most didn't hold onto their losing positions for forty-five years. They sold out, usually at the bottom.

This is not opinion; this is simple fact.

Notice, there were years where the prices went up by thirty percent or more, but they also came down by that much or more the next year. In the end, either you threaded the needle by buying and selling correctly or you lost money. Most people didn't make money, of course. Most people just got scared, ran out of patience and sold out near the bottom. Many of those people swore off stocks for a long, long time.

After the Korean War, the economy got much better. We experienced something we now call a peace dividend. You can see stock prices skyrocketed and continued all the way up until the Dow topped out at around 1,000 in 1964. By that time, stock investors were everywhere. The "nifty 50" were in style, taxi drivers and bellhops were giving out stock tips, and this is where most Baby Boomers' parents jumped on the bandwagon.

After all the time we've spent together, I hope you'd expect those people who jumped onto the "nifty 50" bandwagon, or bought the general market at its height of popularity, made nothing over the next eighteen years.

Again, if they had a specific strategy like goldmining or real estate, they made money, but most investors didn't. They followed the strength, just as the herd generally does.

After hitting 1,000 in 1964 with terrific fanfare, the Dow fluctuated wildly but really only moved sideways. After all the easy-money-seeking latecomers had given up and taken their losses, after inflation had made their money worth less than half what it had been worth, after all the horrible inflation under Jimmy Carter, the Dow finally went above 1,000 and stayed there in 1982.

Fanny: It took them eighteen years to break even?

Dan: Most of them didn't break even, Ms. Gold. Most of them were dead or had sold out at the bottom – or both.

With the end of the Cold War and interest rates falling from 1982 to 2000, another fabulous up period created a new generation of people who believed in making easy money in the stock market. Unfortunately, these investors lost most of it when tech stocks crashed in 2000.

That's why your grandparents didn't want to touch stocks in the thirties and the forties. They grew up in a generation where everybody lost money in the stock market. And this is why your parents felt the same way in the eighties. If you talk to Joe Blow now, he thinks stocks only go up because he lived through the nineties. Considering all the money people have lost over the past five years by being careless and overconfident, it's really kinda scary, don't you think?

Franny: You're saying I have to balance on the wire between the sideways-ness of the market and my commitment to my companies?

Dan: Exactly. You'll get the hang of it. It's a dance.

Franny: Honestly, Dan, do you think that I can ever really learn this stuff? It's so nuanced and full of abstract, or at least large-scale, relationships and those relationships aren't really fixed. It's like parenting quintuplets instead of just one kid. The dynamics are like the constant fail/win, risk/safety, watch/act, hold/release thing. It's involving and you have to really think, I mean think like you have to think when you take a test. No wonder we have a herd. How many people who are used to watching television actually think so comprehensively? It's not like you have a population out there reading Proust.

Dan: Well, that's why you make the big bucks for getting it right! But it isn't any harder than running a business, raising children, running a cab company, finding cures for cancer, and it pays a lot better than those things do. You know, there are a lot of people figuring out computers and taking other types of machines apart and putting them back together. I'd say the percentage of people in the general population who can do well investing in the stock market has more to do with them having the right expectations and going after the right information than it does their ability to engage in complex thinking. I think they can do it.I think you can do it, too. Everything looks daunting in the beginning.

Franny: That's true. I remember how hard I thought massage therapy was. I had to learn all of the muscles and bones and chemical reactors and stress points and peripheral factors. It *was* daunting, and then one day it wasn't. I sort of just "got it."

Dan: Just take it slow. You're young. It's like learning a language, learning to ride a bicycle – like many things you've learned to do with unconscious mastery. First you're lost and suddenly, you've got it. The human brain is a wonderful thing once it gets the confidence and determination to master something. The important thing is to start and understand the basic underlying issues such as the herd, your own adrenaline and the current state of the market. Like I said, Ms. Gold, it's a dance.

Franny: This girl needs to study her dance moves. I'll see you next time?

Dan: Same time, same place.

Franny and Gideon

Franny: So I'm not thinking about Gideon at all. I'm busy with the succulents in the back yard when *Mr. I'm-home-but-I-don't-answer-the-door* shows up. He says, "Hi."

I'm like, "Hello."

"So, what's going on?"

"Just weeding the succulents."

"Did you miss me?"

"No."

"I was in Alabama."

"Your car was here."

"I got a ride to the airport."

"They have airports in Alabama?"

"Yes. My grandparents live there, too. Also, I had some business there."

"What kind of business?"

"It's actually about the investment plan I'm making. It's a mobile HIV testing unit that uses cheek swabs instead of drawing blood."

"Cheek swabs?"

"Yeah, a cheek swab instead of a blood test. It's a long story. Getting men to test for HIV is a big problem. This makes it a little easier."

"That's…thinking outside of the box."

"I found a company that provides cheek swab HIV testing. The laboratory is in Alabama. It's a public company that is expanding to mobile units."

"Hey, why not park the units outside of big sports bars or sports events?"

"Why not?"

"Why not? I like that. I might add it to my life philosophies. So…your car was there, but you weren't home?"

"Yep. Say, now that I'm back, I thought I'd try making my grandmother's chicken and rice recipe. Would you like to join me for dinner?"

"You're cooking? Do you like to cook?"

"I love to cook, and I'm embarrassed to say this, but I love to clean, too. It gives me a sense of order."

"What time shall I come by?"

"Seven's good."

(I don't need to tell you that I was pleased at his invitation. I'm not going to pretend any more than a man would that someone who can provide some of the creature comforts such as a home-cooked meal and a clean house isn't someone I'll look at twice.)

I walk in at seven; he's burning a nice candle. He's actually playing Gal Costa. The place looked very nice. We ate, and he was the perfect host. The best part of the evening, besides his company, was the fact that, other than giving me the big eye, Gideon made no moves at all. I like the Japanese tea approach to romance: nuance, rhythm, pace and symbolism. What's your hurry? That's not a life philosophy, but I'm fond of it. He wrapped a couple of warm rolls up for me to take home. That's very nice. Breakfast at some point in Paris would be the topper. (I like to mix a little Tiffany with my kitsch.)

Massage Session #11

Franny: Yo, Dan The Moneyman. I've still got some fuzzy thinking around the whole "hold- onto-it, don't-hold-onto-it" thing. Which is it? How can I tell the difference? It sounds so vague to me.

Dan: One of the reasons people think they should hold onto their investments over time is because their advisors tell them to. This is what I call the Roach Motel Strategy. You're supposed to check in but never check out. They say things like, "Over the last 50 or 100 years the average return has been eleven percent." This makes you feel as if you should just wait it out. This is the conventional wisdom passed on from one person who doesn't know to the next person who doesn't know. It flies in the face of the picture of the last century I showed you last time.

If you were a tree, holding onto your investments for twenty or forty years would be perfect. Over a 300-year life, you wouldn't have to worry. The market's been perfect for at least 300 years. If you were a person who's fifty, you would be interested to know that the market can spend twenty years without going up, and it does this frequently, as I just finished showing you.

You would be interested to know that there have only been two reliable secular up-trends that lasted fifteen or twenty years over the past century, and stock prices have been simply gyrating up and down going nowhere the rest of the time. That means other than three-tenths of the time anyone who bought and held the general stock market made no money at all. Adjusted for inflation, they got poorer and poorer and poorer. Not only did prices in general fail to rise over time, but if they happened to follow the normal emotional reaction of people in the herd, it was even worse.

Franny: How could it be worse than no gain over twenty years?

Dan: Many of them actually did worse than the market because at least one time they followed the herd and bought at the top and, at least one time they gave into the crowd hysteria and sold at the bottom. So the markets went nowhere for twenty or thirty years at a time, and many of the investors actually did much worse.

So while I believe that over the next fifty years the stock market may offer twelve percent or something in there, I also believe that (an average) man or woman who is fifty-years-old doesn't have the time, the courage or any of the other things it takes to hold onto a losing investment over twenty years. I don't think there's a single person who will actually do that.

I have two more pictures to add to that Roach Motel scenario.

One shows a picture of the sixties and seventies, and you'll see that it looks a lot like the current situation in which it's a sideways movement that doesn't feel like a sideways movement. It's characterized by huge swings of twenty, thirty or forty percent. In fact, it's just like a sideways mountain range that doesn't go anywhere but moves around a lot.

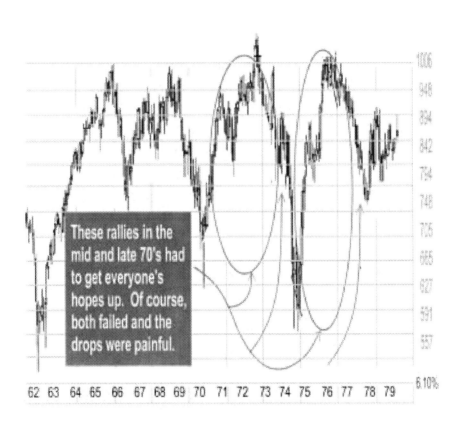

These rallies in the mid and late 70's had to get everyone's hopes up. Of course, both failed and the drops were painful.

If you saw a picture of the stock market from 1998 to the present time, you would see that this is not just a new sell-off that's been going on. We've been in a sideways market with stock prices actually going down for half a decade.

Franny: Bottom line: You're saying that if I don't get satisfactory results in – what? – two or three years – that I should cut my losses?

Dan: No, I'm saying before you commit money to other people's businesses via the general market by buying stock, you should understand that the market moves and is influenced more by the large movements of the herd than by the stories of individual companies and industries. And you have to be open and alert at all times to changes.

In the nineties, you could afford to be patient and very aggressive, too. Even if you made a mistake in timing or you miscalculated a little, the great bull market was likely to bail you out. Most people made money even though they were pretty careless.

In the seventies, there wasn't any updraft. No matter how good a company was, you didn't make money by owning its stock unless you bought and sold at the right time. That's what we call threading the needle. It's not always easy, although you know some pretty good ways to think about it. And by the way, just being aware of this stuff and thinking about it instead of blindly following along puts you ahead of ninety percent of the people who are playing against you in the stock market.

This decade, so far, looks very much like the seventies. Basically, stock prices are moving sideways – some years up strongly, some years down. But in the end, you're only going to make money if you buy at the right time and sell at the right time, or if you use your capital to help people get what they want in a very specific and innovative way.

Franny: Well, what about the China plan you mentioned earlier and the huge increase in the price of oil? The companies in that industry are pretty safe, aren't they?

Dan: You're right that they are in their own private bull market, much like where the technology stocks were in the nineties, but don't kid yourself. A big downdraft in stock prices and a lot of fear among investors will pull down even those stocks. You want to stay awake and take advantage of the herd when you get the chance.

Franny: Jeez Louise, as much rewiring as I'm doing in my brain…It actually is a kind of game.

Dan: Life's a game. You can't take it too seriously. What's amazing to me is the way people enter into a kind of fantasy land when it comes to the stock market. They will begin doing things the way ol' Grandpappy did right after the Alamo, and that method is sacred to them.

Imagine the Indians when they dealt with the cowboys and the

Spanish, and they kept losing the wars. They were completely inundated by diseases. They were almost wiped out. You can imagine the struggle they were going through mentally to maintain their self-esteem as they were being completely destroyed by disease and war. Their cultural mythology is that they are favored by the gods. Imagine when a solar eclipse occurred, how easily it could be used by some shaman or chief to lead these suffering people, to tell themselves that this was a sign of their eventual dominance and victory when all of reality was pointing in the other direction. It's a heartbreaking story, but it shows how persistent man's drive is to fantasize rather than face reality.

Consider this story when you make a desperate effort to grab onto some reason to believe that old story about stocks continuously increasing in value. You are now confronted with the stark reality. It's not a matter of opinion; I'm simply showing you the facts.

Franny: It really is hard for people to change their habits. My great-grandmother always kept a conch shell by the front door in case drunks or wild animals wandered onto the porch when she was alone. She would just blow it loud and long and the neighbors would come from the next farm over. To this day, my mamma keeps a conch shell by the door. She even chastises me for not having one. I'm like, "Mom, I've got a cell phone." People are strange that way.

Dan: Exactly. People need to confront how crazy they're acting, betting their lives based on these vague beliefs. There are bad scoutmasters, great teachers in horrible ghetto schools, and Ms. Gold, there are long periods of horrible stock performance.

When you invest in the stock market you are playing against people who have very sophisticated tools, as I've shown you earlier. While I use big time tools today, I started just like you putting one foot in front of the other, doing research, making a plan and sticking with it.

Be aware that you're going to have to do away with the belief that you're in a stable unchanging world where you can adopt a certain posture and keep it for a long period of time.

You're free to come up with any number of conclusions. One conclusion might be, "It's too hard, and I'm not going to play." I buy that. Another conclusion might be, "I have to be pretty smart because I'm dealing with people who have more information than I do." Another would be, "I love this stuff, and I'll get as much information as anybody in the world." Another one would be, "I'm picking a strategy and working it because I don't have to know and be able to do all things. I only have to do a couple of things very well that work."

Franny: I like that last one. That's the one for me.

Dan: Not long ago, I had an interesting interchange with a young man who became a fan of my radio show. I believe he's in some kind of job that he perceives as a dead-end such as a welding assistant or something like that or he's working in some factory. He's been listening to me, and I've been talking about this herd that influences the market. He's trying to find books to read about it and ways to confirm this. In his quest he's coming across tons of articles in current newspapers and magazines and on the Internet. The problem is that among these current articles many of them are what I call "sponsored" information. They are actually written by people from the large investment houses who are trying to get you to buy their products and put your money with them.

The information he's finding seems to conflict with what I'm saying. He's feeling really frustrated because the stock market has been in an aimless, profitless sideways stage for the past couple of years.

In the middle of this environment, this young man is surrounded by people who are all losing money, including him probably, and he's listening to all of this stuff. He can't really find any information to confirm this, yet it sounds logical to him. He sent me an e-mail in which he's expressing his frustration and turmoil. Instead of answering on the air like I normally do, I actually sent him an answer because I wanted to make sure he got it. I wanted to hold him as a member of the audience. I got into this gut-wrenching conversation with him, and it ends up with him saying that everybody that he works with is laughing at him.

I said, "Why are they laughing at you? Is it because you think that as an American you have half a chance to get somewhere?"

He says, "No, they're saying the only way to make money is to be self-employed, to own a company because everything else is just a rip-off. You just lose money."

I pointed out to him, "What do you think I am doing when I invest in a company? I'm a person taking ownership in a company." The thing that's so interesting to me is that the people who are trying to learn about this have completely lost sight of what they are doing. They're thinking of the stock market as a casino, and they're intent on trying to find a magic bullet in a 3,000 dollar piece of software that simply gives them the ability to get free money. They think it's like a directory of where the easiest girls to pick up on any week night are. There is no such magic bullet, but it's so pathetic to know that people are still looking for one. Certainly, there will always be a 3,000 dollar software package to buy every time you turn around because manufacturers know you want a silver bullet.

Franny: It's like a mantra that you keep repeating over and over again: "Get down and dirty. Do the work yourself, and *you* will make a profit. No one will do it for you. There is no easy way to the yellow brick road."

Dan: It actually is easy – like speaking English or riding a bike. At first, it feels difficult and then you realize it's harder not to do it. You're just not used to using those muscles yet. Speaking of muscles, could you work on my calves? I had to stand for over two and a half hours at my son's soccer game last night.

Franny: Not a problem. When I was a kid up in Michigan, we played soccer day and night, but it was always indoors. I couldn't take the Texas heat. Sea-kayaking may seem like an odd sport for someone who lives in Texas, but I find that it takes me to island environments. When I'm in an island environment, I'm fully Franny, if you know what I mean.

Dan: Environment is not only a key to sanity; it's also a primary method for making money in the stock market. What I'm talking about is actually being aware of your environment. Part of that is to know what the herd is doing at all times.

I spend hundreds of thousands of dollars a year on information to help me follow the market. But what am I supposed to do if I can't spend that kind of money? What should someone like you do?

First, be aware of your environment. Be conscious that the stock and bond markets are just our society's method of allocating capital and deciding which deals are going to get done.

In other societies, the same decisions are made by a commissar, a king or a central committee. So far, having some powerful people deciding which deals will get done and which endeavors will receive the resources has not proven to be the most efficient way for society to build itself. That's why our country is winning against everyone else and always has.

As it turns out, our way of having the free market decide is imperfect, but it's the most successful method that's been tried on our planet so far. Students call it "the invisible hand," but it's really just millions of people doing self-interested things. Essentially, they're trying to figure out the best way to use their capital to help people get what they want.

In our society and in free markets, we reward people for helping others get what they want. The market is our society's mechanism for everybody placing their vote and moving their money to where they think they're helping people get what they want. If you help millions of people get what they want, you can become a millionaire.

If you're investing ahead of everybody else, if you're doing it at a time when no one else sees or wants it, or if everyone else is afraid, then you can see what people want and use your capital to help them get it. You make money. The earlier or more alone you are, the more money you make.

This young guy I was talking to has 20,000 dollars to invest and can't possibly compete with someone with a lifetime of Wall Street experience and every resource in the world. What I can say to him is, "If you can figure out a couple of things that you understand about society and try to take your capital with courage and stick-to-it-iveness and all the things that make America great, use your capital to help people get what they want, the world will reward you. The stock market is the way you do that."

Franny: I like that. I like that a lot. I love basic maxims that you can live or invest by. "Help other people get what they want." That makes sense.

Dan: Exactly. Another way to look at it is to think of the stock market as simply a way to open a store in a good location. When you go into business via the stock market, one of the nice things is that you don't have to go to work at your store. Somebody else is doing the work and watching the money. There are regulators making sure that, for the most part, you are getting the facts and, for the most part, nobody's running away and stealing the money. It's not perfect, but it's better than what you're likely to get if you go out on the street looking for somebody to help.

Franny: Courage. So, Dan The Moneyman, would you say that you're brave? Would you say that if someone has made a lot of money on the market that they're brave?

Dan: Anyone who is successful in life possesses courage. A mother or father with a grown child has a badge of courage. Ultimately, investing a lot of your own money successfully means facing yourself, your fear, your needless anxieties and your passions. Courage, or bravery, is a relative term, but we all have some.

Franny: You're modest. I'd like to step out there and accept the challenge. I'm going to do it, too.

Dan: Good for you!

Franny: That's it for today. Thanks for the inspiration. Say, my neighbor Gideon would like to meet you sometime.

Dan: I don't see why not. This is your partner?

Franny: Yes, you could say that. I'll see you next time!

Dan: Goodbye, Ms. Gold.

See APPENDIX 2 for a more complete discussion of The Roach Motel Strategy – *You get in easy, but you never get out alive.*

Points

- Over the past century, the stock market has seen a couple of fifteen- and twenty-year long bull markets, where just about anyone who participated made good money.

- Almost two-thirds of the time, over the past century, stock prices have moved sideways to down. These bear markets have persisted for decades, and people who invested in the Dow stocks or in the general market did not make money unless they bought at the right time and sold at the right time.

- At times, during bear market decades, even great companies that were competing successfully saw their stock prices decline severely. During the secular bull markets, investors made terrific money on stocks of companies that were not actually competing effectively.

- Before you commit money to other people's businesses by buying stock, you should understand that stock prices are often influenced more by large movements of the herd than by the stories of individual companies and industries.

- This decade, so far, looks very much like the seventies. Basically, stock prices are moving sideways – some years up strongly, some years down. But in the end, you're only going to make money if you buy at the right time and sell at the right time.

- Drop the belief that you're in a stable, unchanging world where you can adopt a certain posture and keep it for a long period of time.

- Avoid directly competing with the pros who have more money and information than you have. You don't have to know or master all things. You only have to do a couple of things very well that work.

- Evaluate the information you use based on who you got it from and what their agenda is likely to be. Understand the biases that are often part of sponsored information you get in media or on the Web.

- If you want to get better as time goes on, keep a journal or spreadsheet that records which expert recommends what and when. Record how accurate each expert is over time. You will develop favorite sources of information that work very well for you.

- Remember that as the environment changes, one or another expert falls into and out of rhythm with the markets. Also one or another gambit or strategy you develop falls into or out of rhythm with the markets. The game changes all the time. Knowing this and remembering it will give you a huge edge over almost everyone else.

- Be aware of your environment. Be conscious that the stock and bond markets are just our society's method of allocating capital and deciding which deals are going to get done.

- Use your capital to help people get what they want. The earlier you spot these opportunities, the more profitable they will be for you.

- Know that none of these opportunities remains a good deal forever. Success attracts capital, which pushes prices up. Eventually the prices reflect all the potential profits and more. At these euphoric moments, have the discipline to sell. Avoid giving back your profits once you have earned them.

- **Be at peace with the fact that you can never be actually on time for anything. You are always either early or late. "On time" lasts only a millisecond. You will almost always either leave some money on the table or sell late and lose back some of your profit. Make sure you decide in advance, in your written plan, which of these you are planning to do.**

Franny and Gideon

Franny: I'm getting curious about what Gideon's up to with his investment plan. I mean, he knows all about mine. Parity is a big thing with me. Not that I have to always have everything be equal. Like if I were married and my husband broke his back, I would wheel him around or adjust his traction. He might just squeeze my hand or make me laugh, which would be fine. Parity, for me, is about letting down your guard, not what you give or don't give. I just wanted to know what makes his heart beat. When I ask him, he says, "Blood."

"Very funny," I say.

"No, really. I'm passionate about blood. I think blood products and supplies are important. I think virus-free blood is important. Blood is the stuff that courses through my veins, literally, and figuratively."

"That's eerie that we're both so biologically oriented."

"Is it eerie or is it synchronistic?"

"That's where you're putting all your money, these swab stations?"

"That and a hemoglobin product that replicates blood that can be stored easily and used in substandard conditions. I found a company in Germany."

"Between us, we're saving the world, aren't we?"

"No, we're just giving people what they want, like Dan The Moneyman says."

"I'm starting to like you."

"Ditto."

At this point, I wondered if I should confess about how I'm really a blue-eyed blonde and not a green-eyed red head, but the moment passed. The blond aesthetic idea has been bugging me. If he's so *not* into the dominant culture in this country, then does that include me? Tracy Chapman says, "Consume more than you need/This is the dream/Make you pauper/Or make you queen/I won't die lonely/I'll have it all pre-arranged/A grave that's deep and wide enough/For me and all my mountains o'things." Am I, by circumstance of birth and by choice, a part of the dominant culture? Deep down, I think it's a yes and no answer. It's confusing.

Gideon and I are just joking around these days. A second date has not presented itself. I think that he's meditating more, and so am I. I'm certainly sitting on my bed listening to the sound of the ocean waves on my CD a lot.

Actually, I came to some thoughtful conclusions in my quiet space, and I'm not really able to contain conclusions very long, so I called Gideon on the phone.

"Gideon?"

"Yes. Franny?"

"Yes. Hey. I've been thinking, and I'd like to run these thoughts by you. Do you mind?"

"Not at all."

"It's like this. You and I are white, middle-class Americans. If you think about us or if I think about myself in that way, I feel terribly guilty. I could just be swallowed up by the weight of it all. On the other hand, Gideon, I really *like* me. I mean, I like my skin, I like my hair, which is blonde by the way. I like my brain and all of my parts.

"Listening to Dan The Moneyman, I realize that for me as a world citizen, it is not unlike me as an investor. I've got to be awake, I've got to step away from the crowd and I've got to have real faith in myself."

"OK."

"I'm just telling you this because I know you are sick of the blond aesthetic, and I'm blond and I have blue eyes, and I think what you really mean is that you're sick of the way people turn a certain look into a Gold Visa or a Platinum MasterCard: deep credit based on looks. I don't think that you actually care more about an aesthetic than you do the person. Am I right?"

"I think, Franny, that as hokey as it sounds, we are all one. I believe that. I think that every choice we make affects someone else. We're Americans, and that's the reality of being American. I think that you are beautiful from the inside out, and your aesthetic is your love of life."

"So…we're copacetic?"

"We are."

"So…great. (pause) I'll see you later then."

"See you later, Alligator. Thanks for sharing. I appreciate it."

"Bye."

"Bye."

Massage Session #12

Franny: Good afternoon, Dan The Moneyman. How is life treating you today?

Dan: I can't complain, Ms. Gold.

Franny: Well, I want you to tell me more about how you choose the companies you invest in. I mean, I'm going along with my little plan, but I think that down the line, you may not be around when I have to make a more complicated decision.

Dan: To a very large extent, my biggest commitment is to the BizRadio Network to which I am basically committing my life. I believe that it is the most direct way to help people get what they want. My commitment there is much larger than any commitment I'm making to any other companies or stocks. To an extent, I'm betting small on guessing where the herd goes, and my large bet is helping people get what they want. I think for the most part, people can imitate most of what I do. Depending on how courageous and insightful they are, they can become very wealthy.

I can tell you that prices are falling all over the world as we speak. I know that billions of people all over the world are intent on moving from the country to the city, and I know that there's no despot or political system that will be able to stop them from this. They all know how we live. They've all seen American television. They've all committed themselves to getting what we have for their families. I promise you that no one will be able to stop them from doing this.

Billions of people in all parts of the world will be entering the middle-class over the next five to ten years, maybe sooner. To do that they have to have automobiles and air-conditioning. They'll need a lot of stuff that you and I take for granted right now. In order to get it, they'll use iron, steel, petroleum and copper. There's no question – this will happen.

When the trick was software, it was possible for someone to find a bunch of kids in Austin that could program a computer and make a company and sell stock. When it comes to finding copper deep in the mountains of South America with bulldozers the size of your house, it's not that easy to get into business.

For the companies that are in the business of doing that, there's no question that there will be some spotty or lumpy stock performance and that the price of these stocks will fluctuate. An academic way of saying this is there will be cycles, with prices rising and falling, within the secular bull market for these building blocks of society. The attractive companies to invest in are those involved in finding, processing, transporting, storing and using all the rare things that it takes for a farmer to become a middle-class urbanite.

In addition to my BizRadio Network commitment, I want to provide capital for financing the acquisition, funding, moving, processing and storing of copper, iron, metallurgical coal, natural gas and things like that. I'm especially interested in special materials like uranium for nuclear power and titanium for air-planes, golf clubs, hip replacements and a thousand other uses. I'm betting that those will be good businesses to be in. I still believe that in spite of the fact that people are nodding as they hear this they will be surprised at how profitable those companies will be compared to a lot of other industries.

You may be joining me at a time when it's already done and over or at a time when optimistic expectations about the world economy has driven those prices up too high. If that's true, be patient. A round of panic and fear about the economy slowing down or some other similar worry will create another favorable entry point for you. The principle of my thinking remains valid.

Franny: So, you're motivated by two factors: what the less-developed masses want and what the middle-class masses do in the stock market.

Dan: Yes, to simplify it. You need to know two things to create profit: 1) What is the herd doing? 2) What does the world want and need? At times when the stock market is so inundated with fear of a slowdown that people are selling everything including the companies that are finding iron in South America, I can take advantage and buy those shares at a fraction of what they were going for when investors were euphoric.

I'm ruthlessly willing to buy as people panic. In that case, I don't have to time it perfectly because nothing will stop the growth of the middle class all around the world. There are ups and downs on a small scale, but later in 2006, I think it will get much worse, and at that time, I will commit large amounts of capital to companies that find, store, process and transport raw goods. I don't think it requires hundreds of thousands of dollars worth of data processing, and I don't think you have to be that smart to execute this strategy.

Franny: You say you've committed your life to BizRadio. Why is that exactly?

Dan: My message is about not getting conned instead of how to use a silver bullet. The silver bullet is really this: If you can go through life in America without getting conned, you ought to end up rich. Just look around you. The value of everything around you is increasing in value at twelve percent a year, and you're not. So you ought to get rich if you just stop doing whatever you're doing.

What I've been telling you, Ms. Gold, are the confessions of a hired gun. I think I always knew how to make money, but I didn't always know how few people get to participate and how few people understand what is happening to them, as they get screwed. That's what I learned from being a hired gun: methods of screwing people. I'm about revealing how it's being done to you and millions of other people.

Franny: Tell me then, what are some resources besides the Internet where I can get the real skinny?

Dan: I can tell you to take the technical analysis that you can buy in a shrink-wrapped box with a huge grain of salt. Basically, this leads you to follow trends and look for trend lines and corridors. Often this stuff is faulty and unreliable. Sometimes it's worse than useless because once thousands or millions of people are looking for the same formations, they simply stop working.

I would advise you to learn about the normal technical analysis tools and use them to veto something. In other words, if I wanted to buy something and I looked at the chart and if it was in a classic negative spiral, I might wait but I would never use any of those standard technical tools to decide how to commit my money.

I'm telling you more about what your state of mind should be and how you should go about getting the exact information.

Here is a specific almanac tip that will help you a great deal. It flies in the face of what a lot of people are telling you, but it is absolutely confirmed by high-class research which has been duplicated a number of times and which is guiding much of the world's smart money.

First of all, one of the biggest determinants of what goes on in the marketplace is the price of money – interest rates. You're buying stocks for money. The government regulates money, and the Fed regulates interest rates in the United States. Because so many countries have economies that are tied to ours, the Fed is, de facto, regulating the entire world's economy. This is even more important now than it has been in the past.

In the past half-century or more, there have been periods when the Fed was tightening or raising interest rates by pulling money out of the economy – actually, out of the banking system. There are times when the Fed was lowering interest rates by putting money into the banking system and thereby, putting it into the economy. They call it "printing money," but what they're doing is pouring money into the banking system. During the past half-century, the Fed made interest rates go up or down about fourteen times.

During all of the times when the Fed was raising interest rates, the return on all stocks, as a group, has averaged near zero. Individual sectors may have done well, but I'm talking about the whole market – what most middle-class investors buy – what a diversified portfolio of mutual funds is made up of. During these rising interest rate periods, prices have been very volatile and investors have suffered very big losses. On the whole, if you simply owned stocks during the time that the Fed was raising interest rates, you made no money, which means you lost money due to inflation.

During the times when the Fed lowered interest rates and poured money into the economy, on the average, over my entire lifetime and I'm sixty-years-old, the average return on *all* stocks (not stocks picked by me and not smart stocks, but *all* stocks) has been about 2.5 percent per month. The volatility has been much lower, and you have been heavily rewarded for investing in innovation, so that would be a guide to you: If you just played the game when they were lowering rates and got out when they were raising rates, you'd have been a helluva lot richer.

Franny: I believe you. I'll need to do more reading on it, but I mean you are a sort of walking advertisement for your way of thinking, aren't you? It's like Marilyn Monroe push-up bras. Who wouldn't buy them?

Dan: I find you very refreshing, Ms. Gold.

Franny: Why, thank you.

Dan: I'm glad you said you need to do more reading. You may want to trust me, but go and find out for sure. Practice vigilance.

Those people telling you to hold on all the time are *simply lying*. They should know better, and they do know better. There have been people who won Nobel prizes for telling you to hold on. Their work, their institutions have been sponsored by insurance companies and other people who get you to put your money with them while they collect fees and commissions. If you only knew whether interest rates were moving up or down and acted accordingly, you would be infinitely richer.

Remember when the Fed lowered interest rates in 2001 and 2002 to try to pull us out of the recession they had just created? The stock market didn't pick up immediately, but it did eventually. As they were doing that, people were saying, "Oh, my god, it's not working this time." Eventually, it always works. The Fed always gets its way. By October 2002 the stock market was beginning to stir, and by March 2003, we were in a full-scale bull market.

On average, the numbers I'm giving you are accurate and will probably continue to be so over the next fifty years. It's very important for you to remember this. When somebody tells you to take a big stock position while the Fed's raising interest rates and tells you to make long-term stock investment, you know they either don't know what they're doing or are lying. It's that simple. Remember: There are always exceptions. For example, while the Fed has been raising rates over the past couple of years, gold and raw materials stocks have soared.

Franny: I'm following you. When the Fed raises interest rates, long-term investments are a bad idea. This is so obvious. I just don't get why the experts on TV and in the newspapers weren't shouting, "Danger, keep away!"

Dan: Because there's a time lag that they just don't see. When the Fed puts money into or takes money out of the system, it takes between nine months and a year for the economy to respond. Most people without a lot of experience just don't understand the time lags, so they say things like, "The Fed's raising rates, and it just isn't working."

What's really true is the effect hasn't had time to show up yet. Trillions of dollars have been lost by a lot of very nice people by making this particular mistake.

There's an old saying that the function of the stock market is the orderly transfer of assets from the poor and uninformed to the rich and well-informed. And much of this transfer takes place at turning points.

Remember Y2K? The Fed started raising interest rates in August 1999. It started raising rates and markets faltered a little bit, but because Alan Greenspan was worried about Y2K, he started flooding the market with money again. Right after January of 2000, he raised rates again once he saw we were safe. The stock market crash occurred in March 2000.

At the time, the Fed had been raising interest rates for months and tech-stock prices were still very strong. People were saying "This time it's different. It doesn't matter what the Fed does because these tech companies don't borrow money."

They forgot that if people in regular industry have a big slow-down, there won't be anyone left to use all that software. The fact is that the cycle occurred as I described; it just took a while – a perfect example of "the time lag."

Then, once the Fed lowered rates again in 2002, the same thing happened in reverse. People said, "The Fed's lowering rates, and it just isn't working." The spring of 2003 was one of the best moneymaking opportunities of our generation. Everything was in place to make the economy take off, and most regular people just didn't expect it. Those who understood the simple mechanics made a fortune. I talked about this earlier when I told you my story about the duct tape.

The good news is we're going through the same predictable process right now, and later in 2006 or in 2007, we'll have another beautiful, low-risk entry point growing out of another Fed tightening episode that eventually worked.

Franny: I remember the first science fiction novel I ever read, *War of the Worlds*. After that, it was like a light came on: There is fiction beyond the realistic. I plunged in and never looked back. That's how your explanations seem to me, Dan. I'm getting a perspective that will change my landscape.

Dan: Fantastic. Remember I talked about helping people get what they want? Instead of having that in mind and using the stock market to deploy their capital, people in 2000 were overinvesting in a few companies that had already attracted too much capital. Everybody in the world tried to invest money in those few companies. Investment bankers were desperately promoting and even creating companies left and right to meet the demand for technology stocks, and investors turned into a huge herd, mindlessly searching for a free lunch. They never even thought about helping people get what they want.

Franny: It's funny – most catastrophes that happen to us can be traced back to us.

Dan: Funny. Actually, people lost all those trillions of dollars because they missed a couple of basic principles.

First, they just jumped onto the bandwagon and poured money into stocks that were already inflated by demand overpowering supply. Pouring more money into those tech companies didn't help people get what they wanted.

Second, when the Fed started raising interest rates, investors didn't pay attention and felt bulletproof! At the very least, they should have said, "Well, I'll ride it but watch out carefully for the inevitable end, which has to be nearby. When I see the signs of weakness, I'll jump off. This is neither what the stock market is about, nor is it what the economy is about."

Understanding these two simple thoughts would have saved many ruined lives: 1) Help people get what they want, and 2) Watch the interest rates.

Franny: It seems so simple, doesn't it?

Dan: It is that simple!

Think about what happened in 1929. That was when we had a classic set-up in the market. Everyone agreed the bull market would go on forever. Everyone agreed the economy was fabulous and threw all caution to the wind. A few people saw signs that the general herd was all invested out, and these people started to sell stocks short. With few buyers remaining, prices started to fall. Once they tasted blood, these marauders kept selling. People who borrowed money to buy stocks were the first to be wiped out, and the losses exploded! The short-sellers kept selling. The careless herd created some very rich men that year but many millions of poor ones.

Many people don't know this, but the President of the United States asked these few people to stop selling short for the good of the country.

Franny: Did they?

Dan: Of course. Some things are more important than money, but that is a little background on short selling.

Franny: Did you do short selling in March 2000?

Dan: No, but somebody did. I could see it so clearly.

Franny: So you think selling short is the best strategy for me?

Dan: No, Ms. Gold, not really. It is an important tool to use when people are too exuberant and overconfident and blindly buying everything in sight. But with productivity exploding and Asian buyers just entering the market these days, there are too many good opportunities to pass up.

Franny: Well, it's always good to keep history in mind, just in case.

Points

- A secular bull market exists for companies involved in finding, processing, transporting, storing and using all the rare things that it takes for a farmer to become a middle-class urbanite. Materials that are the building blocks of new society will be in demand for many years to come.

- Within this secular bull market, there will still be cycles. There will be periods where euphoria will have driven materials prices and stock prices unrealistically high. As an investor, you will want to lay off at these times and may even want to take profits and wait for a new entry point.

- The American and the global economies will also take a rest sometimes. Human psychology being what it is, these inevitable slowdowns will often be accompanied by panic "sky is falling" predictions and temporarily falling materials and stock prices. These will serve as low-risk entry points along the way.

- It's alright to learn what you can from simple-formula, technical analysis tools that are sold everywhere, but you should take this pop culture stuff with a grain of salt. Remember: When you know what everybody else knows, you know nothing.

- During all of the times when the Fed was raising interest rates, the return on the total stock market has averaged near zero. Prices been very volatile, and investors have suffered very big losses. On the whole, if you simply owned the general stock market during the time that the Fed was raising interest rates, you made no money, which means you lost money due to inflation.

- During times when the Fed has been lowering interest rates, the total stock market has returned well over two percent per month!

- Obviously individual sectors and companies can buck these overall trends, as goldmining shares have bucked the current sideways trend.

- **When somebody tells you to take a big diversified stock or mutual fund position while the Fed's raising interest rates, they either don't know what they're doing or are ill-advised. It's that simple.**

- **When the Fed manipulates interest rates by adding money into or taking money out of the system, it takes between nine months and a year for the economy to respond. Many mistakes are made by investors and advisors who don't understand this time lag.**

Dan's Thoughts

It's hard for me *not* to keep history in mind. Sometimes, I think I *am* history. In the past ten years, just like in the twenties and thirties, we've seen the best of times and the worst of times. But because of the productivity of our time – because our lives are dominated by information technology – the highs are higher and the lows are milder than they were in the twenties.

In 1995, the market began to change, much like it did after WWI. The conversion of investors to the stock market was on. It was time to simply ride the wave. Investing in individual companies wasn't as important as simply participating in groups of stocks through mutual funds and exchange traded funds. Not much homework was necessary. You just had to make sure you didn't get in your own way. The supply/demand situation created rising stock prices and rich investors for the next five years.

Then March 2000 arrived. The Federal Reserve had been raising interest rates, tech companies had been using their inflated stock as currency to purchase other "dot-coms," and there was an excessive supply of stock on the market from all of the Initial Public Offerings (companies selling stock to the public). This created a nasty recipe for future stock prices.

Three years later, the market finally found a bottom – investors had lost thirteen trillion dollars. Most investors expressed

224

hope that they had seen more volatility in those seven years than they would ever experience again in their lifetimes. It was one of the best bull markets in history and one of the worst bear markets in history, back to back. A tale of two markets was finally over.

In 2004 and 2005, we entered into what I consider to be a normal market. You should expect:

- The trend for the overall market is generally sideways.

- The major averages have reasonable ups and downs.

- It's smart to take profits when stocks get ahead of themselves.

- It's smart to buy companies that provide goods and services that the world needs when they are on sale.

- Buy and hold doesn't work except at certain special moments in history. We are not in one of them at this time. Deal with it.

I've tried to give some insight into the kinds of information and techniques the best and the brightest on Wall Street have at their command. The average investor is not going to be able to compete effectively on a level field.

Instead of trying to play even against the major leaguers on their own turf, a much better idea for the average investor is to become as knowledgeable as possible in just a few areas. Understand the economics, the competitive issues, and make yourself familiar with some of the companies in your selected areas.

I'm going to give you a start by pointing out five basic areas that deserve your attention. With very little time and effort expended, you can give yourself a terrific edge by learning as much as you can about some or all of these five areas.

There are several companies and mutual funds mentioned in this report. They may have been or will be owned in the past, present or future for accounts that I trade in. Be very clear that companies mentioned by me or anyone else should not be purchased just because a well-written, articulate report mentions them. There are also macro and technical reasons not to own these five areas from time to time. But all in all, I can assure you these areas will be held in my portfolio most of the time over the next decade.

#1

Let's start with healthcare. The first thing we know for sure is that human beings are living longer than ever before. There are several reasons for this.

- Better medical care and healthier lifestyles – especially a drop in the smoking rate
- Safer cars
- More women starting prenatal care earlier in pregnancy

For these and many other reasons, the number of people sixty-years-old and older is increasing very rapidly. In fact, people sixty-five and older represented only 12.4 percent of the population in the year 2000. According to the Administration on Aging, they are expected to represent almost twenty percent of the population by 2030, almost seventy million people. The number of individuals eighty-five and older is estimated to increase to almost ten million by 2030. Baby Boomers are the "meaty part of the curve" in our population.

I'm interested in the companies that will help keep our aging population's blood pressure down, our hair growing and our skin looking young. Consider companies that manufacture artificial hips and knees, treat Alzheimer's disease, and run assisted living facilities, home healthcare, home modification and adult daycare.

One company that can help with the artificial hips and knees is Zimmer Holdings, Inc. (ZMH). They engage in the design, development, manufacture, and marketing of reconstructive orthopedic implants in the United States and internationally. The company offers reconstructive orthopedic implants, including joint, dental and spinal implants, trauma products as well as related orthopedic surgical products. Zimmer's orthopedic reconstructive implants restore lost joint function due to disease or trauma in knees, hips, shoulders and elbows. This is a twenty-billion-dollar company that is growing by leaps and bounds. After a huge run up in 2002 and 2003, investors are getting a great opportunity, as the stock has been flat since the middle of 2004.

United Healthcare (UNH) is a company that provides healthcare services to fifty-five million Americans. With the aging population and Social Security in the situation it's in, Americans will be working longer. UNH provides plans to businesses large and small across the country. This is a steady company that has provided steady growth for several years. It's a seventy-billion-dollar company that is expected to grow fifteen percent in 2006.

Medicare reform has been on the table for some time – it will kick in and be in full gear in 2007. Prescription cards will mean more people will have access to drugs they need. The most likely beneficiaries will be the retail pharmacies. Two of my favorites are Walgreen Co. (WAG) and CVS (CVS). I think there is enough growth to go around for all pharmacies to benefit.

Many of the best healthcare companies can also be considered technology companies. Two of my favorites are Merge Technologies (MRGE) and Laserscope (LSCP). Merge is a software company that develops e-film for doctors. Gone are the days where the radiologists held the film to the light to show you the fracture. As with other technology, radiology is moving toward digital. Merge has a product called PACS, a system for storing, retrieving, and viewing X-rays, CT, MRI, nuclear medicine, and ultrasound. Another Merge system, RIS, is a specialized system that supports radiology charge for billing, storage of patient data, scheduling, and reporting.

Laserscope (LSCP) is a new favorite of mine. I especially love the fact that investors are passing on it, and the stock price is languishing (as of this writing). Laserscope engages in the design, manufacture, sale and service of medical laser systems and related energy devices for the medical office, outpatient surgical center and hospital markets worldwide. The company's product portfolio consists of lasers and other light-based systems for applications in the urology, dermatology and aesthetic surgery markets. I like this one because of the many uses for its products. Given that almost everyone knows someone who has died of prostate cancer, it's awesome to see a product that can actually help ease an enlarged prostate. These lasers can also be used in hair removal, leg vein solutions and acne treatments . This company has the power to help Baby Boomers look better and live longer.

#2

The previous companies are a perfect segue into my second crucial area, technology. Technology has been and will be a part of our lives forever. Because of technology, the world is smaller now. We're able to communicate with people around the world instantly. In fact, my company has constant video communication going on, just like the starship Enterprise. It's as though whatever city we're in, we're in the same room. In addition to the thousands of dollars we save every year in travel expenses, it saves us time, allowing much greater productivity. Technology has made us a more efficient and productive society.

Because everything I do is so information-rich, I can proudly say that the work I can accomplish now, in one day, would have taken a whole week and an entire staff just a few years ago.

The first tech area I want to focus on is the "guts" of almost all technology. Semiconductors are at the heart of technology and key to our economy. Semiconductors aren't just in our home personal computers. They're in our cars, our televisions and even our refrigerators. We've noticed in the past few years that a rally isn't really a rally unless semiconductor companies participate. The biggest and best is, of course, Intel (INTC). This is a company I've owned on and off for years. It's a cyclical business like most others. But this is a dominant company in one of my five crucial areas. It's worth over 165 billion dollars in market cap.

A lot of people will argue that Intel is just too big to grow. That is true of many companies. They simply get too big and can't produce the type of growth that justifies paying a lot for the stock. But companies like Intel have a lot of resources, namely cash. They can use this cash to acquire fast growing companies (their competition), or they can use it for more research and development. These companies have a lot of intellectual property that isn't accounted for in their earnings, which is why P/E ratios are meaningless with technology companies. Intel can withstand downturns in the economy because it can still pay its employees and survive even when times are tough. And right now, we are going through a product cycle upgrade. Most corporations haven't upgraded since the Y2K exercise. Intel will benefit from this.

One of my favorite things about Intel as an investment is the very thing that makes it such a money-loser for so many people. The fortunes of the general semiconductor industry and the price of Intel stock is extremely dependent on the economic cycles we go through. Because the company is so strong, and is in the middle of every new invention and technology upgrade, it is the perfect stock to buy from panicked investors at the bottom of the cycle and sell back to euphoric, overconfident investors at the top of the economic cycle. I think of myself as having an Intel store, where I buy the stock wholesale and sell it retail, and I get to do this over and over.

Next, focus on consumer electronics. This is a fast-changing area, and we're in the middle of another product cycle upgrade. Consumers are shifting from analog televisions to high-definition digital televisions. If you've been in a Best Buy lately, you'll notice that "regular" televisions are tucked away in the corner. Most of the shelf space is dedicated to brand new, flat-panel, large, high-definition televisions. The High-Definition Multimedia Interface (HDMI) is the evolving standard in home-theater technology. It is the first and only industry-supported, uncompressed, all-digital audio/video interface between components. HDMI provides an interface between any audio/video source (e.g., a set-top box, DVD player or A/V receiver) and an audio and/or video monitor, such as a digital television, all through a single cable. This eliminates the need for all the tangled wires. The company at least a generation ahead of its competition in this area is Silicon Image (SIMG). It's almost a billion-dollar company and is right in the middle of the analog-to-digital transformation.

I'm usually involved in a lot of discussions about Best Buy. And even though I'm a big fan of Best Buy, it's still a company I wouldn't want to own as a technology play. Yes, it's the biggest and best and that's where everyone goes to get their new "techy" stuff. But it's still a retailer, and there's not much to stop other companies from selling the same things. In addition, they have huge competition from the online world such as Ebay. I would rather own technology that can't be duplicated, like specific semiconductor companies and software companies.

Do not be lulled into a sense of false security as an investor in technology. If you want slow, long-term commitments to specific companies, stay out of this sector completely. Technology is an area that has to be traded because the product cycles are so short and new competitors come into the mix all the time.

I wouldn't hesitate to buy an exchange traded fund or a mutual fund, but don't be fooled into thinking you have reduced your risk and can continue to hold on. This group was once thought to be immune to the business cycle. Remember: That mistaken belief alone cost investors trillions of dollars. If you are willing to deal with constant change, one fund is RS Information Age (RSIFX). This is a very volatile fund that is like the end of the tail on a dog.

A quick digression: This is a perfect opportunity to bring up the self-defeating way most investors are trained to buy mutual funds. If you look for the one-, three- and five-year track records of funds to help you decide which one to select, you will be moved to buy a volatile fund like this RS only when it is at the top. That's when you should be thinking about selling it. The second part of defense is anti-terrorism stocks. These are companies that can make software, X-rays, image detection systems and more. Because this is such a new area, there are a lot of small companies doing some really neat and important things. But they are too small and too speculative to mention in this report. Half of them may go out of business while the other half may thrive. There are a few, however, that are bigger and more established.

First is L-3 Communications (LLL). This is a ten-billion-dollar surveillance company. It should be a core holding for a defense portfolio. It's one of the big boys.

The second company is CACI International, Inc. (CAI). This is an information technology services company serving the Department of Defense. They are supposed to grow at over twenty percent per year over the next five years.

Next is a company in the business of infection prevention, or defense against bio-terrorism: Steris Corp. (STE) is a two-billion-dollar concern that not only helps with prevention; it also helps with responding and recovering from bio-terrorism. This is another company that does many things in the anti-terror area not directly related to defense, but it's a large company that is established and a solid grower.

The last is a company that provides solutions for human identification. Knowing who's coming and going in airports and subways is more important than ever, and these guys have software that can identify through a huge database exactly who's who. This company is Visage Technology (VISG). Of the four anti-terrorism companies mentioned, it is the smallest – less than 300 million dollars. If you are ever going to buy a fund like this one, you should buy it when it ranks near the bottom in performance. Remember: You are buying into a sector, and you are doing it when you believe it is on sale.

Many of the anti-terrorism stocks pop on any terrorism news. That's not the time to buy these. Buy them on pull-backs and when they've nailed down some long-term contracts. Keep an eye out for smaller companies that I haven't mentioned. Someday, they'll be safe enough to buy.

When the market goes up, RS will tend to move twice as fast and vice versa. It concentrates in smaller companies. If you want a non-managed exchange traded fund, you can look at the iSHARES Goldman Sachs Technology Fund Index (IGM), which concentrates in larger, more established companies.

#3

One thing September 11, 2001 taught investors was the huge risk none of us had ever factored into our analysis – terrorism. We all knew about interest-rate risk, economic risk and political risk, but we didn't know about terrorism risk. Personally, I think we were skating on thin ice for years without knowing it. Terrorists have actually been attacking U.S. assets around the world since the seventies. In 1992, when the World Trade Center was attacked the first time, it should have been a huge red flag, but it wasn't. Almost ten years passed before our collective carelessness came back to bite us. We now realize that defense applies not only to our country but also to our portfolios. Defense companies are not only a good hedge against terrorism but also a sound investment due to the global landscape and the sad realities of the world we live in.

Because our country under-funded the military in the 1990s, there is some catching up that has been going on. This will continue. Defense spending is currently between three percent and four percent. In addition, replacement of aging equipment will be necessary in the years to come. But the main bullish influence on this sector is the war on terror. The long-term commitment we've made to beat terrorism will keep defense spending high, and staying at war will keep the U.S. government in the spend mode, replacing all the items it takes to run a war (tanks, bullets, gear, etc.). There is also a strong move to replace manpower-intensive battle techniques with high-tech solutions. Fortunately for smart investors, this involves spending money instead of lives. There are budgetary concerns that loom over this sector, but I believe there will be plenty of money allocated to defense regardless of the new budget numbers. Under the Bush long-term plan, funding for defense will increase to about twenty percent above the average Cold War levels by 2009 (adjusted for inflation).

First, there are the defense contractors. There are the usual suspects like Boeing (BA), Lockheed Martin (LMT), Raytheon (RTN), General Dynamics (GD) and Northrop Grumman (NOC). These are the big boys. They provide the essentials to the defense industry, from fighter jets to navigation and radar systems.

But if you're looking for a couple you haven't heard of before, there is AAR Corp (AIR) and Orbital Sciences Corp (ORB). Both of these companies are expected to grow their earnings by almost twenty-five percent per year over the next five years, yet the stocks are selling very cheap compared with others. Orbital Sciences Corp. develops and manufactures small rockets and space systems for commercial, military and civil customers. Some of its products include interceptor rockets and defense satellites. About fifty-four percent of their revenue comes from the Department of Defense and intelligence agencies. Also, I've noticed a lot of insider buying in this company.

AAR Corp (AIR) is a diversified global company that provides aircraft and engine parts, maintains aircraft, develops structures and systems, and even does aircraft sales and leasing. This is a company whose customers include not only the U.S. Government and Department of Defense but a lot of the big defense contractors mentioned earlier. One thing to consider is that only about forty percent of this company's sales are to the defense industry; the majority is commercial aviation.

Both of these are smaller companies whose stocks have been strong recently. But if you want something with more upside potential, these are two companies to consider.

Fidelity does offer the Fidelity Select Defense and Aerospace Fund (FSDAX) for those who want a fund instead of individual companies. But this fund can be just as volatile as some of the stocks mentioned. As with the stocks, I'd wait and buy the dips, as the fund tends to run up a lot at certain times.

#4

One of the best money makers throughout the recent global growth cycle has been in the resources area. It's no secret that prices in the United States of gas, copper, cement, coal, etc., have been in a long-term up-trend. There is one reason for this – global consumption is likely to outpace supply. China and India are industrializing; they don't want to ride bicycles anymore – they want cars. They're building huge buildings and laying roads. These things take tons of resources and there's simply not enough to go around. In fact, there hasn't been a major oil find in over thirty years. Unlike technology companies, companies that provide resources like copper and titanium are easier to invest in because their story is simply based on supply and demand. For the next decade, there will be shortages, not only in the industrial materials I mentioned but also in agricultural commodities like sugar and wheat. Like technology, this area is subject to wild price swings. In April 2005, when there was talk that U.S. economic growth was slowing, these stocks saw their prices fall twenty percent in some cases. That type of volatility won't end. That's why it's important to have a bias to own these – but there will be times to take profits. I owned Intel (INTC) in the nineties several times. Yes, I could have just hung on. But I slept better at night knowing I was taking profits when everybody loved it, and I was buying it when they said tech was dead. These companies are no different. Let's start with a few names of individual companies, and then we'll go into some mutual funds.

One that I like is Monsanto (MON). Everybody may know this company because they make Roundup, the weed killer. But, they're more than that. They make genetically altered seeds for farmers. These seeds are resistant to bugs and droughts. They will see a lot of growth in China and the rest of the developing world over the next several years. This is a large, stable company that has had a big run the past two years. But it'll pull back like they all do, and that will be your opportunity.

Let's move on to iron. The largest producer of iron ore is Companhia Vale do Rio Doce (RIO). This is a company based in Brazil that is bringing iron to the rest of the world. Most of it is going to China. This is a volatile company that should be bought on any fears of a slowdown, either in the United States or globally.

An even better opportunity for a better and longer term deal will come in late 2006 or in 2007, when the global economy really does slow. Beneath the surface, I see signs of this slowdown, but the investing world is not seeing them yet. RIO and others mentioned here will likely experience huge price declines, and this will eventually provide us with a real, high-profit, low-risk entry point. Buying these stocks when the investing world is overreacting to the slowdown could be one of the easiest and best opportunities of this decade.

This opportunity is the flip side of a real chance to lose a lot of money. This will happen to many investors as they get caught holding these materials stocks when the world finally starts to notice and react to this global slowdown. You do not want to get caught holding these stocks when this happens because you will feel like you're being carried right off the cliff. Do not try to be the last person holding these volatile stocks before they take their dive, and do not try to be the first one aboard as they recover. There will be plenty of time. Note that the economy will decline in late 2006 more than people now expect, and the shock will mean stock prices plummet. But the economy may not decline as much as the panicked investment world will expect, and therein will lie your opening for a couple of really profitable years as the sector recovers on into the 2008 Presidential election.

This plan applies just as well to the rest of the stocks in this section. Copper is an essential element to the industrial materials world. There are lots of copper companies, but my favorite is Southern Peru Copper (PCU). This is one of the more volatile copper companies, especially compared with the bigger Phelps Dodge (PD). But volatility doesn't always equate to greater risk. This company has a bright future and a dividend of over ten percent.

In the oil and natural gas area, I like XTO Energy (XTO), a fast-growing mid-cap company that is taking advantage of the energy bull market. As oil swings back and forth, so does the stock. It should be bought on dips. Recently, the company was hit by a scandal, which though very limited, has brought the stock price down severely.

Probably the best business model in the natural gas business belongs to Chesapeake Energy (CHK), also to be bought on the dips that seem to come around twice a year.

With oil topping sixty dollars a barrel (depending on how quickly I can type), alternative energy plays will become more important over the next several years. One that I like is USEC (USU). USEC supplies low-enriched uranium (LEU) for commercial nuclear power plants worldwide. This is another volatile company that can be traded but has a lot of growth potential. USEC is the speculative uranium stock; Cameco (CCJ) is the pure play – the low-hanging fruit, if you will.

If your style is mutual funds, two that I like are the RS Global Natural Resources Fund (RSNRX) and the Oppenheimer Real Asset Fund (QRAAX). The RS Global Natural Resources Fund will give you a lot of exposure to the energy market but also has holdings in some of the stocks mentioned above.

The Oppenheimer Real Asset Fund (QRAAX) will give you exposure to more of the straight commodities like sugar.

Just like the stocks in the group, these funds aren't buy-and-holds. It's too volatile of an area to just buy them and put them away for years. They should be sold or at lease partially sold when everyone agrees that resource companies are the place to be and they should be bought when you start hearing that oil is going back to thirty-five dollars per barrel.

#5

Let's shift gears now and talk about something that everyone understands and likes – income. The four previous areas all have to do with capital gains. The nineties made everyone feel like they didn't need any income in their portfolio because capital gains investing (stocks mostly) was making over twenty percent per year. Who needed lousy old boring income? The early 2000s reminded everyone why income should be a major part of everyone's portfolio. When September 11, 2001, came, people exited stocks and prices fell. Guess where that capital went? That's right, the bond market. It's often called the "flight to quality." That means "Get me out of the scary stuff and put me in the safe stuff – even if I only make a few percent, at least I get my principal back." That can also be referred to as a hedge. When my stocks go down, my bonds go up. This isn't always the case. In fact, most of the time, stocks and bonds move together. But a lot of times, when people get scared enough, they choose bonds for the guarantees. For the "flight to quality" reason, they move in opposite directions, keeping your portfolio more stable so you can sleep better at night.

The conventional wisdom currently is that long-term interest rates are about to rise, and that this rise may persist for several years. These are the same things people told us five years ago, three years ago, last year, and so far it hasn't been true. The long bond has been at the current level off and on since the early Clinton years.

Harry S. Dent, the noted author and frequent *MoneyMan Report* contributor believes interest rates will stay low for most of the rest of this decade, as does chief Fed economist Dr. Michael Cox. Cox, incidentally, was nominated for Pulitzer Prize for his observations on our economy, not to mention being a senior advisor to the group that is charged with actually determining rates. Our safe investing plan does, however, provide for rising rates. In spite of some of the luminaries who predict the opposite, we see higher long-term interest rates as a distinct possibility.

Another piece of conventional wisdom revolves around the fact that bonds are a bad deal when rates rise. Let's deal with this misconception right now.

Bonds are unique as investment instruments because they always carry a guarantee that they will be redeemed by the issuer. Dealings with the issuer of a security take place in what is called the "Primary Market."

Dealings between investors on exchanges and elsewhere are called the "Secondary Market." In the "Secondary Market," bonds sell for whatever a willing buyer and a willing seller agree they are worth at any particular moment. Brokers tend to focus with their clients on the Secondary Market because they are most interested in people who buy and sell assets frequently. Long holding periods do not make transaction-oriented brokers any profit at all. Note, though, that the investment banking firms they work for invest their own money as well, and that they do this in a far different way than they suggest to you.

In the Primary Market, bonds are redeemed by contract. If they are callable, they are redeemed at 1,000 dollars each, and when they mature, they are also redeemed at 1,000 dollars each. No matter what they are selling for at any given moment in the Secondary Market, they always fetch the same 1,000 dollars at redemption. The only thing left to worry about is the ability of the issuer to pay the debt on schedule.

Bond traders and brokers do their work in the Secondary Market. Rising rates cause bond prices to fall as they did early in 2004. Conversely, falling interest rates cause bond prices to rise in that market. Traders who expect rates to fall, buy bonds in the hopes of selling them to other investors at higher prices, and when they expect rates to rise, they can profit by selling the bonds short.

This type of speculation is fine, but it is exactly like speculation in stocks. You buy pieces of paper in the hopes of selling them to another investor at a higher price. The risk? You may be wrong.

The retail world of brokers, mutual fund companies and insurance companies is totally centered on the search for capital gains – buying pieces of paper in the hopes of selling that paper to someone else at a higher price. So, it's natural that most investors remain oblivious to the fact that capital gains investing is only part of the investment story.

The very rich, old money families, banks, insurance companies, and major corporations, are determined to stay rich. They would never leave all their money at risk, depending on the vagaries of crowd psychology, political manipulation and international strife. Much of what "smart money" invests in is contractual fixed investments characterized by guaranteed return of capital and contractual interest payments. Armed with generations of experience using their enormous wealth to stay rich and powerful, they lock in their deals right from the beginning. Why? Because they can, and so can you.

Terms are all set in advance before a penny is actually invested. They know how much is put in, how much they get back, how much rent they will be paid for their money and what equity kicker they will get, if any.

Why don't you ever hear about any of this?

Most of you get your investment information from sources that are supported and even created by financial institutions and their representatives intent on furthering their own agenda – selling their financial products. The news is all about capital gains, but the actual experience of investors is far different.

Though they continue to focus on trying to beat the bank by investing in stocks, the truth for about ninety-nine percent of investors is that they have made just about all of their money by negotiated agreements. These negotiated agreements include salary, rent on rent houses, employment contracts and consulting contracts. All these are contractual deals which are negotiated in advance and include the length of time the contract is to stay in effect, the compensation and all terms. All suspense is taken out of these deals and during the term of the contracts, it doesn't even matter to either party what market trends are. Each deal is set in advance until the end of its term, when it can be renegotiated.

Next year, a new basketball player will probably sign a contract for more than this year's top earner makes, but if he's smart, this year's star won't waste his energy worrying about it. The deal is set.

The whole point of making a lease or an employment contract is that neither side has to worry about market trends during the term of the agreement. Suspense is eliminated. At its best, this type of contract locks in a win-win situation. Both sides get what they want, and the deal has a happy ending.

All these deals can be seen as different types of bonds. In this broader sense, bonds include employment contracts – you rent time and skills; real estate rentals – you rent geographical space; and traditional bonds as you already know them – you rent money. There are two types of bonds where we feel we can make the most money over the next few years: **bonds for income and bonds for capital gains.**

Bonds for Income

While it is very profitable and gratifying to our egos and lots of fun to be right all the time, we don't want to bet our lives or our life savings on our ability to time everything correctly all the time (capital gains investing). So we have developed a long-term plan seeking double-digit returns which poses little risk to principal (income investing).

One type of bond we use for income investing is the mortgage bond. These are bonds that are based on pools of mortgages and can pay double digit interest with very little risk to principal. These bonds typically pay interest and principal on a monthly basis. They are analyzed by average life, not maturity. The average life of this type of bond has been less than two years recently. However, with rising rates, we are already seeing the life expectancy of these bonds move further out, to around five to ten years. Longer average lives on these bonds mean more interest and less principal, which raises your overall yield.

As rates rise over the next couple of years, we will continue to buy new bonds. With bond prices falling, we will be paying less per bond and earning more income. Note that if the new bonds are more attractive and pay more because their prices have fallen, our existing bonds will have fallen in price as well. Some of our bonds may show to be worth 800 to 900 dollars per bond. However, you will get 1,000 dollars at redemption, and your monthly cash flow will increase. So, these lower prices are only temporary. Watch cash flow on these bonds. Also, these bonds aren't traded in the Secondary Market on a daily or even monthly basis.

Sometimes the actual market values may drop. However, we are willing and even pleased to accept these interim price declines since we will be buyers, not sellers, and our goal is to double our money over a period of six to ten years with minimal risk. We accept, and even welcome, fluctuating prices. Since we are not seeking capital gains and do not plan to trade these bonds, we will be comfortable in the knowledge that they will each bring 1,000 dollars at maturity or when called (monthly), and we are happy earning nine percent or more as rent on our capital.

Eventually, the economy will soften and the rates will fall. We may even earn some capital gains on the last bonds. For the most part, our strategy with these bonds is to a earn high income and double our money every six to ten years.

Bonds for Capital Gains

In September 2002, with no sign of improvement in the economy or the stock market, many corporate bonds were priced as if the underlying companies would never make a profit again. So we purchased several solid companies' bonds. Many were convertible bonds. Convertible bonds are bonds issued by infant companies that have to add a teaser to compete with other companies' straight corporate bonds. These bonds offer the benefit of converting to the underlying stock. This gives the investor the ability to get potential stock market-like returns with the benefit of at least getting interest every six months, plus 1,000 dollars per bond at a maturity date. At that time, the convertibility was almost irrelevant, because the stock prices were so low and the yields to maturity were in most cases over ten percent per year when you figured in interest plus the built in capital gains (bonds were selling at a discount). Over the next several months, we enjoyed huge returns on corporate bonds. These returns were way in excess of what one would expect to make in a few months on a fixed-income investment.

By early summer 2003, we were focusing on a new type of convertible bond. Coupons were not as attractive, but the bonds provided a good deal of upside potential because the underlying stock had room to grow.

With the improved economy, the corporate bonds have risen in price to such an extent that we have sold almost all of them at this point. As the prices rose, the yields came down, so that we believed there was very little profit left on the table, if any.

As conditions change, we will again try to buy these types of bonds at a discount for high-return potential.

This bond strategy works great because, regardless of what point you're in the economic cycle, there is a bond that works. With an economy that's strengthening, mortgage bonds have higher yields and offer excellent safety. If the economy slows down, corporate convertible bonds go on sale and can be bought for seventy or eighty cents on the dollar in many cases. Either way, achieving close to double-digit returns with a high degree of safety is there for the taking.

For more information on making money with bonds, go to

http://www.escapefromtheherd.com.

You don't have to tell the future to invest safely in the bond market. If the economy continues to strengthen, rates will get high enough eventually to get excellent deals on mortgage bonds. If the economy slows, we'll get our chance in the corporate convertible bond market. In the meantime, we continue to purchase bonds with high single-digit returns and safety of principal and take advantage of these interest-rate swings. The following chart is a picture of one of the ways we watch interest rates swing like a pendulum. We measure the intensity of the moves (bottom frame) which helps us see if we're closer to the top or bottom of any given move. My research also shows that every 200 days interest rates tend to make a significant bottom.

Nobody can tell the future. But regardless of what happens, there is no doubt that the world will need technology, defense, healthcare and natural resources. Our job is to figure out which companies will be the best at providing these goods and services to the world and to profit from them. And we create cash every month from our income portfolio to take advantage of the temporary dips in these areas.

As with any investment, there are going to be times over the next few years when these areas will go out of favor. We want to lighten up when people get too optimistic about these areas and buy when they feel it's over. If we stick to that strategy, we can both make big money over the next few years.

Franny: Um, I think you just earned yourself about ten free massages, Mr. Frishberg. You have launched me on my journey, Sir. I thank you very much. More than anything else, I've realized that I've just been a passive patsy and playing a victim's game. You really woke me up to my own Isis qualities.

Dan: My pleasure, Ms. Gold! Remember: If you think it's a sure deal, your best bet is to do nothing.

Franny: Got it! That's it for today. Will I see you next week?

Dan: Same time, same place. Oh, let me come out and meet this Gideon fellow.

The 200-day cycles of interest rate bottoms.

10-Year U.S. Treasury Rates

200-day cycles

Franny and Gideon

Franny: Gideon and I huddled down and set up a regular business meeting to go over our plans. He encouraged me to travel to Thailand, and I actually have the trip set up with a kayaking detour.

The second date turned out to be a Japanese Festival of Lanterns in Clear Lake. He had his arm around me. I whispered in his ear, "It's like a fairy tale. I wish it would last."

He turned and looked into my green-tinted-blue eyes with his green ones. "Fairy tales are fun, but we have to stay awake."

I took a mock-serious tone with him, "There's no short- or long-term escaping. That's the rule! We *have* to stay awake, we have to be vigilant. We have to watch out for the herd, bulls and bears and crazy investors and…"

"And what?"

(I was going to say Dynasty Son Syndrome but I didn't.) "Nothing. That's all, that's all I can think of right now. But really, Gideon, it is like a rule to follow above everything else: Pay attention!"

"I have another rule I like even more," he grinned wickedly. "The Golden Rule."

I won't even tell you that he kissed me because you know he did. This is the beginning of me, Franny Gold, winning in love and rolling in dough.

The End

Appendix 1

The Crazy Investor Indicator Report

<u>Why timing matters now more than it did a few years ago</u>

Interest rates, after falling for twenty years, are now likely to stay level or rise. Periods of rising interest rates are the most risky for stock or bond investors. And now, the climate for stock prices is still challenging, given a war and high commodity prices. Periods like this one have lasted for whole generations in the past. Times like this have proven difficult to invest in broad-based indexes if you don't have a reliable timing tool.

The persistent and reliable rise in stock prices during the eighties and nineties was, to a large degree, a product of the falling interest rates and the peace dividend that accrued from our winning the Cold War. This type of positive stock price performance has never occurred during times of war or when interest rates have been on the rise as they are likely to be now. During today's challenging times, the last thing we want to do is to risk our hard-earned money matching wits with brilliant, rich MBAs on Wall Street, in control of all the information in the world and carrying few psychological weaknesses. We're interested in low risk and high rewards, and the best way to achieve those is by taking candy from the proverbial baby. This isn't our hobby.

We're investing our life savings, and this isn't a game we're willing to lose!

In search of the low-risk buying point

The reason investing in complicated times is fun is that making money during these times is more a function of psychology than it is math. Human beings are herd animals. We have noticed, as I'm sure you have, that smart people are often dumbed down when they act as part of a group, mob or herd. Think of the towns-people in a movie when they form a lynch mob. Think of political demonstrators screaming about global warming or throwing bottles at the police. Remember: These people really know very little about global meteorology, and most of them are law-abiding citizens most of the time.

We've observed over the years that when investors begin to act as members of the group or herd instead of as individuals, their group nature can be awakened and they can often get carried away with the group's ideas and fears.

Notice that the tool described in this report – we're aptly calling it the Crazy Investor Indicator – has led us to identify seven great low-risk entry points over the past four years. Each one has proven extremely profitable.

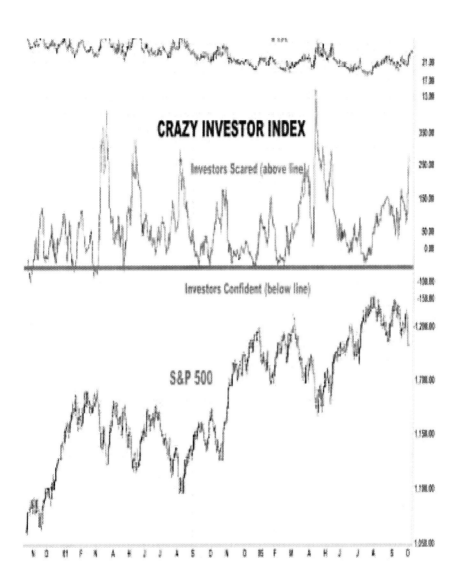

<u>Here are the specifics:</u>

To have our way with the crowd, we have to identify those times when normally intelligent individual investors are being swept away by crowd psychology. Because it's not practical to ask 200 million investors how they feel, we've worked very hard over the past several years to come up with a way we can understand the crowd's psychological state by inference.

The most accurate we've been able to come up with over the years is based on some assumptions. We continue to honor these assumptions simply because of how accurately the indicator has worked. Here's our thinking. The craziest investors in the world are options traders – investors who pay a premium to speculate in the options market. These options are highly leveraged, extremely volatile instruments that actually disappear into thin air if you hold them too long.

We've often been able to gauge how scared, irrational or crazy investors are feeling by measuring the activities of options investors. We can infer their level of desperation from how much these highly emotional, often inexperienced speculators are willing to pay for a basket of options.

This measurement of investor panic or euphoria is called the Index of Implied Volatility. Although this is logical, experience has shown us that this data does not, by itself, give us clear signals. But we have found that we can process the data using a measurement called the Commodity Channel, which compares the highest and lowest levels over a given period to give us meaningful data. In this case, trial and error has led us to observe the Index of Implied Volatility through a 100-day Commodity Channel.

For those who really want to get technical

Our Commodity Channel level is calculated by determining the difference between the average level of implied volatility and the average of the average level over some number of days – in this case, 100 days.

This difference is then compared to the average difference over the same time period to factor in the volatility of our basic index. The result is then multiplied by a constant that is designed to adjust the channel so that it fits into a normalized range of about +/-100.

Warning: Here's a very important point– we use this indicator differently, depending on whether we believe we are in a bull or bear market!

During a bull market, moments of maximum fear and panic by the herd identify profitable entry points but do not give good sell signals. During bear markets, the reverse is true. During bear markets, moments of overconfidence or complacency, identify good selling or short-selling points, but you'd be promptly buried by trying to follow buy signals.

Appendix 2

The Roach Motel Strategy

The biggest and most widely accepted Wall Street Lie of our lifetime is the idea that timing – making appropriate investment decisions by responding to the world situation – is unimportant and unprofitable.

It is not hard to figure out who is responsible for spreading this story. Realize that in buying this logic, you are left with no course of action other than to buy and hold high commission mutual funds and related investment packages such as funds wrapped in life insurance policies (called variable life insurance and/or variable annuities).

This is what I call the ROACH MOTEL STRATEGY. You are supposed to check in but never check out.

After a twenty-year brainwashing campaign matching the intensity of anything the Marxists ever came up with, 100 million middle-class American investors believe that holding a group of large companies forever has been an effective retirement plan throughout modern history.

Ironically, I've had this fiction recounted to me as fact by countless attendees at my personal appearances, even though a simple check of the history books reveals a far different set of facts. Even if you studied the history, as I have to keep perspective, it helps to step back every once in a while and actually look at the evidence. This chart shows the prices of the Dow Jones Industrial Average each year since World War I.

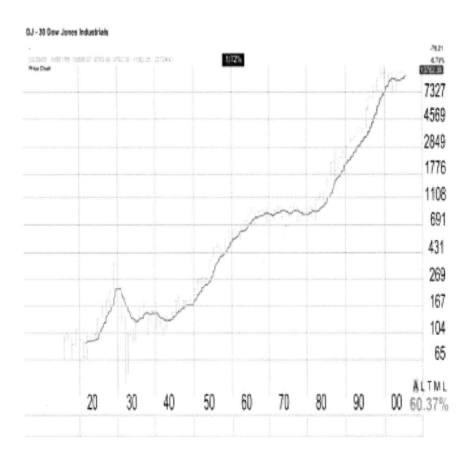

In my quest for understanding, it helps me tremendously to compare the actual stock prices to their five-year moving average. Because free charting generally doesn't allow you to see this far back or to generate a five-year moving average, you hardly ever see this publicly.

Over the years though, I've found this comparison of the stock prices of the Dow Jones Industrial Average to their five-year moving average to be a great tool. It really puts the long-term story of the stock market into perspective. Although the mutual fund/variable insurance crowd hopes you believe otherwise, the picture in the chart is clear.

It shows that throughout the past century, sideways-moving, unprofitable stock markets, lasting for as long as twenty-five years at a time, have alternated with twenty-year bull markets in which buying and holding was a strategy that worked quite well.

The five-year average is such a useful tool and provides so much clarity because during the long periods of stagnation, the Dow Jones Industrial Average (pictured as bars, each representing one year) moves up and down, crossing above and below the moving average line. But during the good times, the Dow prices stay above the five-year average and never touch it. It almost seems as though market participants can see the black line, though we know they can't.

Contrary to conventional wisdom, investors have lived through long periods of stagnation alternating with periods of secular strong price performance.

All this makes perfect sense when you notice that the periods of stock price stagnation come during periods of war, global political turmoil and restricted trade. The good times have always been associated with a peace dividend.

The story starts in 1914 – the beginning of the "War to End All Wars." Though the mutual fund/insurance companies lead you to believe the stock market has continually appreciated on its own with no management, you can see that stock prices moved sideways all the way through the end of WWII in 1945.

There was an attractive five-year bull market following WWI, which ended in the late 1920s. This was succeeded by an equally steep decline in the early thirties, a.k.a. The Great Depression. After three decades of churning, the Dow was roughly unchanged. In other words, a forty-year-old investor who bought into the buy and hold story, invested in the best companies in the United States and held on to them until he was seventy made no money. Fortunately, nobody held on for thirty years, and neither would you. There really is no such thing as a buy-and-hold investor.

By the end of WWII, in 1945, the United States had become the leader of the Western world. Millions of young men and women returned home armed with skills and excellent work habits and were ready to produce. Technologies that had been developed for war were now available to improve peacetime life, and the government no longer had to drain most of the capital from the economy.

The economy experienced what we now call a peace dividend, and stock prices, which had gone nowhere for thirty years, rallied for the next twenty. Stock prices moved up and down, crossing above and below the black, five-year moving average line until 1950, then moved above that line and stayed above it until the mid-sixties. Stock prices staying above the five-year average is characteristic of the peace dividend rally, and so is investor euphoria and overconfidence, so that by 1964, stock investing was becoming as popular with the middle-class as it had been in the 'twenties. Taxi drivers and bellhops offered hot tips to anyone who would listen, and doctors touted their favorite stocks in the operating room.

Two major events uniquely distinguish the year 1964. The Dow Jones Industrial Average hit 1,000 for the first time, and the peace dividend ended, as Americans were shocked once again to find they were not omnipotent. The Vietnam Conflict was heating up as tens of thousands of our best and most productive men and women were shipped to Asia to fight and lose an unpopular and undeclared war. The government again gobbled up every nickel of spare capital, and the stock market never rose above 1,000 to stay until 1982. For two decades, stock prices languished, with the Dow moving up and down, crossing above and below its five-year average. Again, if you would have bought and held the best stocks you would have made no progress. This time, though, you'd have been miserable because inflation under President Jimmy Carter peaked in double digits. While stocks gained nothing over eighteen years, the market prices doubled or tripled on everything.

Stocks didn't really go anywhere. They had good years and bad years, but they went nowhere. The index moved back and forth, above and below its five-year moving average. In other words, buy and holders made no money. Then when the war ended, the Dow moved above its five-year average and started climbing. All the way until the mid-sixties, the Dow climbed and never got below the five-year moving average. Never touched it. Then it peaked in 1964 at 1,000. This was when we realized Vietnam wasn't going to be a piece of cake. It cost a lot of money, and there was a lot of strife, uncertainty, and distraction. From 1964, the Dow again went nowhere for eighteen years. It had beautiful twenty-five percent years and terrible years where it was down twenty-five percent. People who knew how to ride the good times and avoid the bad times made great money. But if you bought and held stocks, you ended up with no profit, and you had less money in 1980 than you had in 1964. Worse, inflation made your savings worth less than half what it was back in the sixties. Through that time, the Dow moved back above and below its five-year moving average.

But then in the early eighties, Ronald Reagan brought about new stability, pride in being American and new technology emerged. Interest rates fell and the dollar strengthened. Gold steadily declined in value. The Index started a steady move up, and rose above its five-year moving average. Picture that line moving well above that five-year moving average and staying there. Even in 1987, it didn't come close. But at the end of the nineties, you could see the stock prices start to level off. For a little while, as you know, the NASDAQ kept rising, but by late 2001, the Dow moved below that five-year moving average for the first time since 1982. Though we can't predict the future, you can't help seeing that today's market looks very much like the war market of the forties and like the strife-torn market of the seventies.

Remember: There were some great years in the stock market, even during the toughest decades. And if you knew how to ride the rallies, and then avoid the big declines, you made money. It wasn't impossible then, and it's not impossible today. Many people did it very well because these cycles were many months find they were not omnipotent. The Vietnam Conflict was heating up as tens of thousands of our best and most productive men and women were shipped to Asia to fight and lose an unpopular and – even years – find they were not omnipotent. The Vietnam Conflict was heating up as tens of thousands of our best and most productive men and women were shipped to Asia to fight and lose an unpopular and long war.

But if you had no sell discipline, you made nothing. No growth.

We'll have plenty of opportunities to make big money, but we'll have to be wide-awake and on top of our game to make it happen.

If you'd like to know how trading works in a sideways market and how profitable it can truly be, go to www.themoneyman.com and click to receive your FREE thirty-day trial of *TheMoneyMan.com Market Newsletter*.

If you have any questions, want to make an appointment, or want to attend a future seminar, call at 877-342-6999, toll free, and we'll help you any way we can. Good luck and I look forward to hearing from you soon!

~ Dan The Moneyman

Notes

<u>Passionate interests</u>

1.

2.

3.

4.

5.

Notes

<u>Correlation of Passionate Interests to</u>

<u>World/Industry Needs and Wants</u>

1.

2.

3.

4.

5.

Notes

Research Points

Notes

<u>Research Points</u>

Notes

<u>Investment Plan</u>

Escape from the Herd

Secrets of the Super Rich

Escape from the Herd